Godawful

Connections Between Biblical Journeys And Life Transitions

Andre Papineau

CSS Publishing Company, Inc., Lima, Ohio

GODAWFUL

Copyright © 2004 by
CSS Publishing Company, Inc.
Lima, Ohio

Scripture quotations are from the *New Revised Standard Version of the Bible*, copyright 1989 by the Division of Christian Education of the National Council of the Churches of Christ in the USA. Used by permission.

Scripture quotations are from *The New English Bible*. Copyright © the Delegaters of the Oxford University Press and the Syndics of the Cambridge University Press, 1961, 1970. Reprinted by permission.

Library of Congress Cataloging-in-Publication Data

Papineau, Andre, 1937-
  Godawful : connections between biblical journeys and life transitions / Andre Papineau.
    p. cm.
  Includes bibliographical references.
  ISBN 0-7880-2329-2 (alk. paper)
  1. Christian life—Catholic author. I. Title.

BX2350.3.P35 2004
248.4—dc22

                                                                        2004010607

For more information about CSS Publishing Company resources, visit our website at www.csspub.com or e-mail us at custserv@csspub.com or call (800) 241-4056.

ISBN 0-7880-2329-2   PRINTED IN U.S.A.

Acknowledgments

My special thanks to Dan Pekarske, SDS, for the innumerable hours he has spent editing the material in my books. Without his help and encouragement, I never would have entertained the idea of publishing at all. I would also like to thank Norman Merz for his invaluable help as I called on him time and time again to help me on my hazardous journey through computerland.

Table Of Contents

Introduction

There are many journey stories in the Bible, and as many reasons why people journeyed. The Israelites fled oppression in Egypt for better days in another land. Escaping Jezebel's fury, the prophet Elijah hightailed it into the desert, while Jacob abandoned family and friends to avoid his brother's wrath. The Magi were in search of the newborn king, and a merchant sought the pearl of great price. One traveler met with misfortune on his way from Jerusalem to Jericho, while a young man broke loose from home for a life of adventure in a far country. The Spirit drove Jesus into the wilderness to confront Satan, and Jonah grudgingly traveled to preach God's mercy to the Ninevites. Jesus sent his disciples in all directions to heal the sick, and bring great news about God's abiding love.

Although these travelers journeyed for different reasons, they invariably went through a transition of one kind or another. From a spiritual perspective we might view these transitions as conversion experiences because these travelers underwent positive changes in self-understanding, as well as in their relationship with others and God.

By reflecting on our transitions through the lens of these journey stories, and on the journey stories through the lens of transitions, we gain insight into both transitions and stories. For example, reading the Prodigal Son's journey as the story of a stormy departure from his home helps us see our difficult times of departure from a biblical perspective. But viewing the Prodigal's breaking away through the lens of a transition about breaking away enables us to appreciate why he had to do so. We are then doubly enriched because both journey story and transition story speak to us in startling new ways.

A few preliminary remarks on the stages of a transition should be helpful before we see how they are operative in the chapters that follow. Whether we are going through transitions like leaving home, marrying, having children, losing a parent, or retiring, we can identify three phases or stages in transitions: separation, liminality, and reincorporation. Identifying these phases conceptually doesn't mean that we can easily distinguish one from another as we go through our transitions. Nor does it mean that we all go through these stages in the same way. But, these distinctions might aid us in anticipating some of the problems associated with transitions, thereby navigating them more effectively.

Separation is the phase of letting go, of saying goodbye, of grieving. Whether we are getting married or going through a divorce it is crucial to acknowledge and grieve our losses. We are grieving not only something or some other we have lost but also something of ourselves that is lost when we lose the other. Losing something of ourselves can lead to a mild or severe crisis of identity, e.g., I wonder, "Who am I now that my wife is gone?"

Separation is followed by an in-between time. The technical term for this in-between time is *liminality*. In rites of passage or rituals of transformation among tribal societies the novices went through a liminal phase. The word liminal comes from the Latin *limen* which means threshold. To be on a threshold is to be neither in one room nor in another, but in between. The novices in these prescribed rituals entered a liminal phase in which they were no longer children nor were they yet adults. They were somewhere in between.

In our transitions we find ourselves neither here nor there, "neither fish nor fowl," "betwixt and between." A confused teenager is neither a child nor an adult. Newlyweds also, while they may have physically separated from their biological families one or both of them might not have separated psychologically. Or, they might be in the process of separating and therefore remain somewhere in between. In a transition we find it extremely uncomfortable to be neither here nor there in a transition. However, we shall have ample opportunity to discover the importance of this phase of a transition.

During the *reincorporation* stage we begin to see the light at the end of the tunnel. We speak of getting our act together or getting on with our lives. This stage is the culmination of a series of breakthroughs which give us a clearer sense of who we are and where we are going. It is the stage of new beginnings.

These three stages share similarities with tribal rituals of transformation which I alluded to earlier. Tribal members celebrated their transitions as important transformative experiences in which the initiated achieved a spiritual rebirth. They realized what we seldom do, namely, that transitions are often critical times for achieving our own spiritual rebirth or renewal.

The journey stories in the following chapters enhance our understanding of themes that often appear during different transitions in our lives. In chapter 1 the leave-taking and homecoming in the journey of the Prodigal Son is used to illustrate our need to differentiate ourselves from and yet be in relation to that with which we have been identified. In chapter 2 by reflecting on Jesus' journey into the wilderness where he is tested in discerning the source of his worth, we are aided in discovering our worth during transitions when we might otherwise feel worthless. The problems and promises of transitioning into the different communities which assist us on our life's journey is addressed in chapter 3 as we travel with Jesus into the wilderness where he feeds the people who have gathered to hear him. In chapter 4 we consider the transition which occurs when we begin to feel helpless in the presence of others' suffering by attending to how Jesus instructed his disciples to heal the sick on their journey to the villages. Chapter 5 focuses on the transition from finding little or no meaning in what had centered us, to discovering a renewed center of meaning. For this we meditate on the story of the Good Samaritan. Jonah's disturbing journey to Nineveh is the backdrop for chapter 6, understanding our transition from the experience of the manageable, predictable god of our constructions to the unmanageable, unpredictable visitation of Godawful. In chapter 7, by journeying with the disciples on the road to Emmaus, we turn our attention to the transition of moving from a way strewn with illusions, to living the way to which we are called. Finally, in chapter 8, we explore the journey we're on from life to death, namely, the journey to quench our thirst for the infinite as mirrored in the story of the woman at the well.

9

Suggested Exercises — Questions For Discussion

Small groups as well as individuals can use this book for private reflection. If it is used by small groups the members of the group read a chapter prior to each meeting. It is advisable that they read the chapters in the proper sequence since material covered in later chapters often refers to material in earlier chapters.

When the members assemble, one of them might lead the others in the exercises and/or questions for discussions. The amount of time allotted for an exercise depends on the total amount of time during which the group will be together as well as the number of exercises they choose to do, or the questions they would like to discuss. Since the purpose of both exercises and questions is to assist the members to reflect on the relation of the readings to their lives, there isn't any need to cover all the exercises or answer all the questions.

It is important that the members are free to speak or not to speak about whatever they have written in their notebooks during the meeting since one or another person might feel uneasy in revealing what he or she has written. Since privacy is important, the members should agree when they meet whether or not what they say during these meetings remains within the group.

The purpose of doing the exercises within the group is to enable the members to get in touch with the living waters (John 4:14) within themselves, thereby establishing a connection not only to their depths but also to one another. The idea is that the more we are in contact with the living waters within our own wells, the more we shall discover that the same living water flows into all of our wells. The value of speaking aloud what they have written is it deepens the members' connection among themselves simply by hearing one another speaking from their depths. None of the members need comment on what one or another member speaks aloud. There is no need for questioning, interpreting, or even consoling one who speaks what he or she has written. The members are supportive by remaining silent. When sufficient time has been given for the members who choose to speak what they have written, they can move on to another exercise, and/or questions for discussion.

If the members should decide during any session that the questions for reflection are more important than doing any or all of the exercises, the exercises can be dropped.

However, if they decide not to do any of the exercises, they might find it helpful to spend time doing the exercises alone during the week.

Finally, meditation music played during an exercise might be helpful in creating a peaceful setting.

Chapter 1

From Leave-taking To Homecoming

Objective: To have the members establish a connection with the turning points in their lives, thereby achieving a sense of movement through the various transitions which have brought them to where they are today.

Then Jesus said, "There was a man who had two sons. The younger of them said to his father, 'Father, give me the share of the property that will belong to me.' So he divided his property between them. A few days later the younger son gathered all he had and traveled to a distant country, and there he squandered his property in dissolute living. When he had spent everything, a severe famine took place throughout that country, and he began to be in need. So he went and hired himself out to one of the citizens of that country, who sent him to his fields to feed the pigs. He would gladly have filled himself with the pods that the pigs were eating; and no one gave him anything. But when he came to himself he said, 'How many of my father's hired hands have bread enough to spare, but here I am dying of hunger! I will get up and go to my father, and I will say to him, "Father, I have sinned against heaven and before you; I am no longer worthy to be called your son; treat me like one of your hired hands."' So he set off and went to his father. But while he was still far off, his father saw him and was filled with compassion; he ran and put his arms around him and kissed him. Then the son said to him, 'Father, I have sinned against heaven and before you; I am no longer worthy to be called your son.'

"But the father said to his slaves, 'Quickly, bring out a robe — the best one — and put it on him; put a ring on his finger and sandals on his feet. And get the

fatted calf and kill it, and let us eat and celebrate; for this son of mine was dead and is alive again; he was lost and is found!' And they began to celebrate. Now his elder son was in the field; and when he came and approached the house, he heard music and dancing. He called one of the slaves and asked what was going on.

"He replied, 'Your brother has come, and your father has killed the fatted calf, because he has got him back safe and sound.' Then he became angry and refused to go in. His father came out and began to plead with him. But he answered his father, 'Listen! For all these years I have been working like a slave for you, and I have never disobeyed your command; yet you have never given me even a young goat so that I might celebrate with my friends. But when this son of yours came back, who has devoured your property with prostitutes, you killed the fatted calf for him!'

"Then the father said to him, 'Son, you are always with me, and all that is mine is yours. But we had to celebrate and rejoice, because this brother of yours was dead and has come to life; he was lost and has been found.' "   — Luke 15:11-32

"I'm not the same person I was. I haven't a clue what's happening to me." How many times have we heard or spoken these words? Important as they are in disclosing our state of mind, even more important is how we feel saying them. Are we troubled? Fearful of what lies ahead? Do we feel that having known ourselves for years it isn't fair that now we're confused about who we are and where we're going? Or are we comfortable acknowledging an exciting if confusing period of knowing ourselves in a new way?

Often the beginning of certain transitions involves an upheaval in our lives during which we undergo a shift in understanding ourselves and our world. This shift launches us on a journey through which we grow in understanding ourselves apart from, yet in relation to, others. These transitions occur whether or not we consider ourselves, or are already considered "grownups" in society.

Many of us grew up thinking once we had become adults we had achieved maturity. If we accepted this idea, then feeling restless,

14

or anxious, or even a little crazy as adults might cause us to think, "Something is wrong with me; I better see a psychotherapist!" However if maturing means getting psychologically and spiritually bigger, these same feelings might signal the growing pains of breaking through one way of understanding ourselves to discovering another.

There is a pattern in this process. Maturing is a lifetime process of becoming the persons whom we are called to be apart from and in relation to others. In this process we strive to satisfy two basic yearnings throughout our lives: the yearning for autonomy, and the yearning for connection.[1] Both needs are always present but it would be a mistake to identify these needs as opposed to one another, as if maturing meant becoming more autonomous at the expense of becoming less relational or vice-versa. Perhaps a better way of stating how these two needs are met is growth in relationship or the transformation of immature relationships into mature ones through discovering one's self apart from others.[2]

"Apart from" involves differentiating me from what is not me, separating me and mine from you and yours by redrawing the boundaries between myself and the other. "In relation to" means being available or related to others in a way I could not be when I was identified with or embedded in the "Prodigal's Story."

The story of the "Prodigal Son" can help us develop these ideas about being apart from and in relation to. We don't ordinarily think of this story as a story of maturing but it mirrors our journey about leaving home and returning home, about moving apart from and relating to. It is a story with which any age group can identify. Are we justified in looking at this journey story as one of leave-taking and homecoming? Certainly many who have written about the meaning of this parable have interpreted the story as a story of God's gracious, abiding love for those who have strayed from the path and have returned home. Buttrick describes the younger son as "an offensive person" and a "bum" who may be "young and misguided, but he is still a self-centered scoundrel."[3]

However, after considering the various interpretations of this story, Robert Funk dismisses the need to interpret the story morally and sees it as basically one of leave-taking and homecoming. The son has to leave home in order to see his father in a new way:

> The immoderate behavior of the lad and the exaggerated welcome on the part of the father suggest a momentous event in their lives, a turning point: a son cannot know the joys of return until he has suffered a departure.[4]

While leave-taking and homecoming is the context in which we shall view this story, this doesn't mean that we need to exclude Buttrick's negative description of the son. Later we shall see that his assessment of the son is often an apt characterization of someone going through a transition.

As for Funk's dismissal of any religious dimension in the story, since it is simply one of leave-taking and homecoming, we shall see that in these situations there is the potential for spiritual transformation. If by spiritual transformation we mean viewing our world more clearly by differentiating ourselves from others and appreciating new ways of relating to them, then leave-taking and homecoming can be the occasion for spiritual transformation. This spiritual dimension will become more apparent by reflecting on this story and others that follow.

Separation — Leaving Home

The first part of this journey is about the son discovering who he is apart from others. The circumstances in the story help us identify the son as having a wealthy father. How young the younger son is we are not told. The only other information we have about the father is that he has an older son. The young man is remarkably insensitive toward his father. He insists on his inheritance and in effect is asking his father to drop dead! This is psychological parricide.

While we usually imagine the son to be a young man, we could easily imagine a scenario in which the person is a young woman, or someone older leaving home. The biblical story might suggest any situation in which we need the space to arrive at an understanding of who we are apart from others with whom we have been identified. Whatever the circumstances, "leaving home" can be a long and painful process of breaking away. Why is the process of differentiating so painful? Two factors are involved in the process of differentiation: identification and opposition.

Identification

Differentiating ourselves from others presupposes that we are *one* with them (understanding others to include parents, spouse, friends, religious affiliation, and so on). Being identified with the other implies fusion or experiencing life as "we." When we hear someone repeatedly say, "We do it this way" or, "This is what we think" without ever revealing how "I" do it or how "I" think, chances are there is a great degree of identification with the other.

Without being aware of it, each of us is part *of* a whole before we are apart *from* that whole. For example, in the first few months of life we enjoy a symbiotic relationship with our mother, that is, we are one with her, a unit. There are no boundaries between infant and mother. And we don't really begin our journey of becoming separate until the fourth or fifth month of infancy. Then around the eighteenth to the 24th month we go through the period known as the terrible two's as our struggle to be separate and not separate becomes very intense. We want and do not want to be separate. We like being safe but we fear being swallowed up by the mother.

Ordinarily one would think that when people marry they would certainly experience themselves as autonomous, separate persons. But frequently one or both of the partners are still identified with mom and/or dad. Why? Because partners bring to their marriage a host of expectations or mental scripts of how married men and women are expected to relate based on their parents' marital history of relating. Possibly one or both partners might define themselves in terms of the other's expectations and needs. "I am the nice wife or the nice husband if I am what my husband or wife thinks that I should be."

What also militates against differentiation is the romanticized ideal of intimacy: to think as one, feel as one, and finish each other's sentences. We might think it's cute to speak of our "better half," as if two half persons entering a marriage were desirable. The couple might have the illusion that because they are physically separate they have separate identities. But unless they are also psychologically separate they have not fully achieved their own identities.

What it means to be separate is frequently an issue around midlife. "Whose life am I leading? Mine or theirs?" "Theirs" could mean our political party, church, relatives, and so forth, and what they expect us to believe, think, and feel. Acquiescing to others' expectations might be a comfortable arrangement for a while. In the story we can imagine the Prodigal Son surrounded by servants. He has an easy life, maybe too easy. It would be nice to remain at home forever. It's like relaxing in a warm Jacuzzi. Life offers some of us these pleasant situations. Someone else is around making the · big decisions and accepting the consequences. Even if the warm Jacuzzi gets hot we might prefer remaining there and suffering rather than leaving the Jacuzzi to face a cold, unknown future. We resist change because our longstanding identification with the other is the way we have made sense out of life. We interpret our world not through our own eyes but through the eyes of the larger unit, e.g., family, peers, church, and so on.

The process of separating might get underway as we experience conflicting claims to please or not to please others. Being Mr. or Mrs. Nice might have felt good once, but now it has become more and more of a burden. Like the Prodigal Son we also need to break away. Does his father understand why his son needs to leave home? Maybe not. More than likely, his son doesn't understand his need to break away either. Simply because he is having the experience doesn't necessarily mean he has any conceptual understanding of the experience. Later this might occur. But the experience itself might leave him feeling moody, lost, and disconnected from others. Because usually none of those involved understands what is happening, the separation isn't easy.

Opposition

The second factor at work in differentiation is opposition. Initially we "oppose." We oppose ourselves to those with whom we have been identified. Thinking we have been treated as children, we resent family or spouse. Daniel Levinson refers to the late thirties in some men's life as the BOOM or Becoming One's Own Man period.[5] The 38-year-old man feels he is being treated like a child at work when he feels he ought to be treated as an adult and achieve a more senior position within the firm. He is angry at those whom he thinks are preventing him from getting ahead. Like a child he wants the approval of his seniors, but he also wants their recognition as an adult who is autonomous and on an equal footing. In attempting to define himself he opposes himself to the others. On the brink of a midlife transition he needs to rethink what he wants as "opposed" to what others want from him.

During different stages of development and in different life situations we are like the younger son. We too cry, "I've got to go! I want what is mine." Like him we can be aggressive and negative as we struggle to get what is ours, namely, the self that belongs to us. Others aren't necessarily conspiring to prevent us from claiming what we think rightfully belongs to us, but often this is our perception as we struggle to differentiate ourselves from others.

What is happening when we or others are negative or oppositional in separating? By being negative we aren't only saying no to those with whom we had been identified; we are also saying no to something in ourselves. For example, we don't simply say no to parents but we are also saying no to the side of ourselves that had been loyal to them. In saying no to this side representing the loyal son or daughter we are now "losing" what had been a source of our identity.

In the parable it wasn't only the younger son's father who lost his son. The son also lost the side of himself he had always known himself to be: the son of his father. Thus, the decision to leave was not only an act of violence toward his father, but against himself as well. He was opposing the side of himself too closely identified with his father. We can see how radical this oppositional stance is as we begin the journey of finding ourselves apart from others. We too need to lose the side of ourselves too securely identified with others. Then not knowing who we are, we feel lost. Separating or leaving home is about losing ourselves in one way, while returning home is about finding both ourselves and others in a new way.

But the "old me" doesn't get lost so easily. It still makes its claim on the new me, which is asserting itself. That is why I can be angry and defiant as I say no to others, but still feel guilty, disloyal, and cold. The old me, e.g., the nice guy, accuses the new me of being self-centered and cold. We see this clearly in adolescence. In the emerging teenager there is a tension between the me that was identified with the parents (the chubby, sweet, little guy of child-hood), and the me that is emerging (the smelly, smart-alecky ado-lescent). As Dale Olen has described it:

> *Teenagers turn ugly in order to separate from the adults, to become individuals apart from the family. They do not bathe. They have body odor. They wear grubby clothes, old clothes that do not match. They get weird haircuts. They use foul language. They emit gross body sounds at the kitchen table. They appear sullen and bored when visiting the relatives. When they do these things, we need to know our children are performing a function done by the tribe in more primitive times. I would like us to see our children's "turning ugly" as their way of separating from us — a task they need to do in growing up. If we can see it this way, it may help us to become more tolerant of all the strange things they do now.*[6]

The tension between the emerging me and the me that has been around a while can be illustrated in the following dialogue. The emerging me speaks, "I don't want anything to do with people making claims on me. I've had it with people whose opinions and feelings and ideas I've had to put up with all these years. Making it seem like they were mine! Let me run my own life!"

Then the old me answers, "You're out for yourself, aren't you? That's all you care about, not others' feelings. Only what you want! What's wrong with you?" The old me can make the new me feel guilty, especially if the old me has defined itself as a giver. This is why many women feel selfish when they begin to think of their own goals and aspirations in life. Being a giver has been so much a part of their self-definition that many women feel guilty if they pursue their own goals.[7]

So, when the son demands his inheritance and leaves home, he might also be seeking liberation from the side of himself that had been content with a comfortable life — the side of himself identified with his father. This is the side he is losing. Jesus' words that if we are to find ourselves we need to lose ourselves assume new meaning in this context. Understandably we are anxious because in losing the side of ourselves, which we have known, it is unclear how we'll find ourselves again.

This process of losing and finding occurs in marriage, too. As we've noted when people marry they might not come together as separate persons but as persons defined by others' needs and expectations. Traditionally this has been more of a problem for women than for men. Women often came from homes where they had not developed a separate identity, and then entered a marriage in which the husbands' goals became theirs. For many women achieving a separate identity might only happen much later, either in the marriage or after a divorce.

Achieving a separate identity might not take place until one or other of the spouses dies. In some instances, the surviving partner might feel guilty. They might feel that by establishing a new identity they are betraying the memory of the deceased partner. Sometimes, however, the surviving partner might die soon after the spouse because it is so frightening to be left without the "other half" of the relationship. However, in other instances the death of a spouse might even be liberating. The pastor of a church spoke of a woman who had very recently lost her husband and wanted to celebrate this at a Roman Catholic Mass. The priest wondered what she meant by celebrating. She said she meant she wanted to celebrate, to rejoice. She was finally free of him and wanted to enjoy the rest of her life. That was worth celebrating!

Liminality — In-between

After leaving his father the Prodigal Son goes to a far country where he squanders his inheritance. A famine occurs and in order to survive he feeds the pigs. This is degrading and humiliating. If we recall that the Jews classify the pig as an unclean animal, then the modern equivalent is tending rats. What often goes unnoticed is that since he was herding pigs he had to have been hired by a gentile. Borg says of this:

> *He lived in gross impurity and had become, according to the standards of the quest for holiness, a non-Jew, and his father's statement, "This my son was dead," was correct in an important sense: his son had ceased to be a Jew.*[8]

We have called this stage of the journey the liminal or in-between stage because in the middle of a transition we often feel desolate and empty (the famine) as we sink into the muck of a depression (knee deep in pig manure). And like the son we might engage in behavior of which ordinarily we would be ashamed. We might be oblivious to our unkempt appearance, or our eating and drinking habits. Maturing is a messy business. Because our world no longer makes sense, *we* don't make sense. We are anxious and in the dark about what might be happening. Thoughts of dying and even suicide might occur. One reason for this is that the familiar side of one's self (the "old" me, the Mr. Nice me) must die and make way if the tentative "new" side is to emerge.

The son "comes to his senses" only when he is humiliated and begins to despair. He hits rock bottom before he can imagine a way out of his predicament. He imagines being reconciled with his father by mentally rehearsing the words that he will tell him. It's important to note how he is willing to be received by his father. "I am no longer worthy to be called your son; treat me like one of your hired hands." He sees the possibility of relating differently to his father. There is relational distance which enables him to see his father in a new way. This relational distance prepares him for his homecoming.

22

Reincorporation — Homecoming

Homecoming involves recovery and reconciliation. What is lost is found. The father finds his son but the son also finds himself in a new way even as he sees his father in a new way. He is his father's son but he is not only his father's son. No longer is he solely defined by his father's identity. The intimacy, which he now enjoys, is different from the symbiotic relationship he had experienced prior to leaving home.

Earlier we reflected on the fact that intimacy is easily romanticized. We might think people who are intimate share the same ideas and feelings. "We're on the same wave length," or "We're of one heart and one mind." It is a "tea for two" and "two for tea" intimacy. But this is not an intimacy in which two different persons welcome and respect one another's differences. Romanticized intimacy is akin to group think or conformism and the jingoism that often passes for patriotism. Unlike his older brother who remained at home, the younger son returns after having struggled to find himself apart from whatever had been the point of identification at home. He is now capable of some intimacy with his father although he still has a long way to go. His journey is incomplete to the extent that his return was motivated by his need for security. Yet however incomplete, his struggle to find himself as separate and distinct has begun. He has met with some success if we agree with Funk's comments that, "The younger son leaves home in order to come home. He is unable to appreciate his patrimony until he has forsaken it and squandered it. He cannot know his father as parent until he turns his back on home."[9] Simply stated, the Prodigal Son is not the same person he was when he left home.

Looked at as a conversion experience there are many who are skeptical about the young man's conversion:

> *Although the boy seems to have voiced repentance, his supposed conversion may be mostly a "soup kitchen conversion" — he's hungry! His formal recital, "I have sinned against heaven and in your sight," certainly sounds like a liturgical formula, but is said following his vision of farmhands eating well at home.*[10]

However, if the experience of conversion is not a once for all event but ongoing throughout our lives then there is no need to minimize a "soup kitchen conversion." This is especially true if it has even minimally enabled the younger son to relate to others including the cosmos and God in a more objective way. To the extent that he has differentiated himself from what he had been embedded in, is the extent to which he has experienced conversion.

The Older Son

Upon learning of the reconciliation the older son complains bitterly that his father never treated him as he did the younger son. The father responds, "Son, you know that everything I have is yours." The father intends to be reassuring but is he? It's like saying, "We don't have our separate boundaries. What's mine is yours and what's yours is mine." Where there are no boundaries, there are no separate identities. Instead there is fusion or pseudo-intimacy. Genuine intimacy does mean getting close but getting close to one another's differences!

The older brother's story is a story of failed maturity. He stayed home, not out of filial love, but out of a sense of obedience. Now he is upset and disrespectful towards his father. Sometimes we hear people offering excuses for not living their own lives. They complain about an assortment of responsibilities, which require them to stay at home. In some cases this is true but these explanations can also be rationalizations for not assuming responsibility for their lives. These people seem responsible but they might also be avoiding risk. What is revealing is that the older son speaks disparagingly of his younger brother's lifestyle. How does he know what his brother was doing? Is it possible that in his own imagination he was attached to the very same things? Rather than actively pursuing certain goals he could only fantasize them. He never could separate from his father.

Whether or not we leave the source of identification physically, each of us will differentiate psychologically. We need to know who we are vis-à-vis the other however we define the other. Maturing means differentiating, finding ourselves apart from. But of course it also means being in relation to a larger whole. We can call the larger whole the *holding community*. This is a term, which Robert Kegan uses to describe what I would refer to earlier as the relational context, which is so important as the individual differentiates.[11]

Holding Communities

The task of discovering one's self apart from others or in relation to others is either helped or hindered by the kind of support we get. The British psychiatrist and pediatrician, W. D. Winnicott, originally used the word holding when he spoke about how the infant's mother held her child. He didn't mean just physical holding but psychological holding as well. Holding refers to the way in which she cares for her baby. Does she hold her child anxiously? Is she always fussing with the child? Too intrusive? Too anxious? Does she know not only when to hold but when to put the child down, and when to let it be? Holding refers to the whole way of relating to the child.

Kegan took over the idea of holding and adapted it to refer to a lifetime of holding which all of us need as we go through our transitions. As we separate from and get connected to, we need to be held. Children need to be held as they get bigger, but so do married couples. So, too, friends hold one another. Kegan identifies three functions of a holding community: they hold on; they let go; they endure.

Holding Communities Hold On
When the son wants to leave home his father doesn't give him a lecture on how disobedient he is, or how he ought to stay home and be grateful for what he has. This tells us something important. We often feel confused or lost as we begin breaking away from a prior identity, e.g., a widowed spouse, or someone recently divorced. What we need are friends who hold on, who are with us in our confusion. They don't attempt to placate us by telling us to remember the better times we've had. They don't rush in with the

Kleenex. Think of someone whose husband died and the remorse she feels for having gotten into a terrific argument the night before he died. Do we try to fix things, or say it isn't all that bad? Or are we willing to let it be? How do we respond when someone asks where God was when the person's mother died a horrible death? Do we feel we need to defend God, or find consoling words to ease the pain? What is important is simply holding the person through our presence.

Holding on is not holding on to. Holding on to is an attempt to keep things as they were. It is resistance to change. "Before long you'll be back to your old self." Or, "You'll see, time heals everything." Or, "Well, you'll find somebody else." But the truth is: Time doesn't heal everything.

Things never will be the same, and you won't be your old self again. Holding on to assumes that loss, confusion, and anxiety are alien experiences. Yet life is a process of losing and finding one's self. Do we know people to whom we can go who can hold us without holding on to us?

Holding Communities Let Go

We need people in our lives who are allied with the side of us that needs to leave home, even when we don't want to acknowledge that need. Staying at home is a metaphor, a way of speaking about the present arrangement. Leaving home is a way of indicating that it's time to move beyond the current arrangement. People who don't challenge us — who don't "contradict" our prevailing way of seeing and doing things — overhold us. Consequently they prevent us from maturing. We need to assist one another in differentiating ourselves from inappropriate dependencies on others. Otherwise we pay the price of conformity and covert anger or depression. The older brother in the story is an example of someone who became very angry, and ought to have been challenged about his own reasons for remaining at home for so many years.

Letting go tests our capacities for opposition to otherness. If our friends are changing, we are challenged to hold them as they go through their own "nay-saying" stage. Often transitions involve repudiations of previous identifications. They involve anger, hostility, or disillusionment at the church, family, spouse, or work for holding one back. We might be inclined to lecture people who are at odds with previous alliances, especially if we identify with these alliances. Think of people going through a divorce and the hostility they feel toward an ex-spouse, or women who have experienced discrimination in the church. Their transitions are characterized by protest, which is an initial attempt to differentiate themselves from that with which they had been identified. The father in the story permits opposition by the son. He lets go.

Holding Communities Endure

If we want to achieve a separate identity we need to leave home. We need to leave people in our lives with whom we have been identified, and on whom we have been dependent. Yet leaving home is only the first step in the journey. Repeatedly we need to return home to be integrated or reconciled as adults with those whom we have left behind. It is important that there are those who will receive us as the father was there to receive his younger son. Such friends offer us continuity.

Is it asking too much that they be there or that we be there for people coming back home? Are there people who support us as we go through our transitions, as we return from our journeys? Do they stay around after the divorce? After the death of a spouse? After we go through our upheavals? Our crises of faith? Our wild times? Is there a welcoming committee? "You're one of us. You belong. We understand you had to leave, but we want you to know that we're still here for you." Is it being too idealistic to hope there will be people who remain in place for the homecoming? Maybe. But it was Jesus who told us of the father who hobbled down the path to welcome his son home.

We began this chapter with the intention of following the process of establishing ourselves as distinct personalities through the initial step of breaking away from whatever had contributed to our identity. This step is the first step in many transitions and we call it separation, and as we have seen in the journey of the Prodigal Son his task of differentiating himself was a partial success to the extent that he was able to appreciate his father as parent. But he remained unable to appreciate his father as someone with his own distinct personality. In the next chapter we shall consider more fully the liminal phase of a transition as we reflect on Jesus' temptations in the desert.

Exercise

The members spend about ten minutes writing a sentence for each of the significant turning points, which they can recall, that occurred in their lives. These turning points might not have seemed significant at the time they occurred, but in retrospect they were significant, e.g., choosing to work part-time in a store and later becoming the manager, or meeting one's future spouse on a blind date. The turning points might be of a secular or religious nature, e.g., attending AA meetings, which eventually led to a religious conversion. The number of turning points varies with each person. However, limiting the turning points to no more than twelve is advisable. It isn't necessary to write down the turning points in any chronological order.

After about ten minutes the group's leader asks whether anyone within the group would like to speak aloud what he or she has written. There is no need for the members to elaborate on what they have written. Reading aloud (now in chronological order) what they have written is sufficient. The value of the exercise is simply to get in touch with the flow of one's life.

After the members have been given the opportunity to speak aloud what they have written, the leader may then ask the members if any would like to comment how they felt writing or speaking aloud their turning points in the group's presence.

After enough time has elapsed for comments, the group leader might then ask if anything in the chapter for discussion corresponds with any of the experiences associated with the turning points which they had written in the exercise.

Questions For Discussion

1. Recall what it was like when you went through a leave-taking, e.g., going to school for the first time or saying good-bye to a friend or relative who was dying.

2. Can you identify this time as an in-between time of a transition? Was it a time of confusion? Anxiety? Were there mixed feelings? Joy and sadness? Frightening and exciting? Did your feelings about God enter the picture? What were they? Did you feel strengthened or weakened in your faith life?

3. Did anyone help you through any of your transitions? A friend? A clergyperson? Did you reach out to anyone? Could you talk to anyone about what you were going through? Or did you feel there was no one who could help you?

4. Is there anything in the chapter that you found particularly helpful or insightful? If so, does it connect with anything you've gone through or are going through?

---

1. Robert Kegan, *The Evolving Self* (Cambridge: Harvard University Press, 1982), p. 142.

2. Terrence Real, *How Can I Get Through To You?* (New York: Scribner, 2002), p. 166.

3. David Buttrick, *Speaking Parables* (Louisville: Westminster, John Knox Press, 2000), p. 201.

4. Robert Funk, *Honest To Jesus* (San Francisco: HarperCollins, 1996), p. 188.

5. Daniel Levinson, *The Seasons In A Man's Life* (New York: Alfred A. Knopf, 1978), p. 60.

6. Dale Olen, "Turning ugly is part of teens' rite of passage" *The Catholic Herald*, Milwaukee, Wisconsin.

7. Jean Baker Miller, *Toward A New Psychology Of Women* (Boston: Beacon Press, 1986), pp. 48-54.

8. Marcus J. Borg, *Conflict, Holiness And Politics In The Teaching Of Jesus* (Pittsburgh: Trinity Press International, 1998), p. 105.

9. Funk, *ibid.*, p. 188.

10. Buttrick, *ibid.*, p. 202.

11. Kegan, *ibid.*, pp. 113-132.

Chapter 2

From Seeing Ourselves In Others' Eyes To Seeing Ourselves In God's Eyes

Objective: 1) To become acquainted with our personae, and how often we so intimately identify or are identified with them that we can't distinguish who we are from our personae; 2) to consider where our value as persons is apart from the persona or personae, and whether through our desert experiences we can become more aware of what constitutes our real value.

Jesus, full of the Holy Spirit, returned from the Jordan and was led by the Spirit in the wilderness, where for forty days he was tempted by the devil. He ate nothing at all during those days, and when they were over, he was famished. The devil said to him, "If you are the Son of God, command this stone to become a loaf of bread." Jesus answered him, "It is written, 'One does not live by bread alone.' "

Then the devil led him up and showed him in an instant all the kingdoms of the world. And the devil said to him, "To you I will give their glory and all this authority; for it has been given over to me, and I give it to anyone I please. If you, then, will worship me, it will all be yours." Jesus answered him, "It is written, 'Worship the Lord your God, and serve only him.' "

Then the devil took him to Jerusalem, and placed him on the pinnacle of the temple, saying to him, "If you are the Son of God, throw yourself down from here, for it is written, 'He will command his angels concerning you, to protect you,' and 'On their hands they will bear you up, so that you will not dash your foot against a stone.' "

Jesus answered him, "It is said, 'Do not put the Lord your God to the test.' " When the devil had finished every test, he departed from him until an opportune time.　　　　　　　　　　　　— Luke 4:1-13

In describing the Prodigal's journey, I emphasized the difficulties of leaving home or differentiating ourselves from our sources of identification. Whatever the sources are, they have contributed to the way we see ourselves. Basically, we have learned to see ourselves through their eyes. For example, consider some of the sources, which shape this person's self-image:

> *"Hi! My name is Frank Smith. You know my Dad. He's a trial lawyer for a big law firm. You've probably seen his name in the paper. He tells me he sees in me the potential for becoming a great trial lawyer. My mom tells me the same thing. By the way I'm going out with a gal I've known since I was a kid. When I'm with her I feel like a million bucks!"*

A transition that this young man and others like him have yet to experience is discerning what makes him unique or special, not simply as they see themselves through others' eyes, but through their own as well. Stated so bluntly this sounds narcissistic.

But if the question were asked by someone going through a divorce it might be, "Am I loveable and if so, why?" Or if a person's spouse died, "Now that I am alone do I mean anything to anybody?" Or if someone has retired, "Since I'm no longer a teacher will anyone even notice me?"

Unfortunately, during transitions when we are separating from previous sources of identifying our worth or value, we might be tempted to recover our sense of worth in destructive ways. What these destructive ways are will become apparent as we consider the temptations of Jesus in the desert.

Desert Experiences

The desert is the setting for Jesus' temptations. Deserts are classical in-between or liminal settings. They are places where people can easily lose their way and die, as the Israelites discovered in their forty-year exodus from Egypt. Lacking experience, it is impossible to survive in the desert. On the uninhabited sands a person's credentials, reputation, and achievements mean nothing.

"Desert experience" is a metaphor for a difficult transitional period. Among other things it refers to our feelings of loneliness, isolation, and spiritual aridity. Some speak of being confused or lost while others may say they are depressed and disillusioned. Desert experiences can be triggered in many ways, e.g., a divorce, a death in the family, a betrayal, financial difficulties, and so on. But sometimes they just come. We might be puzzled, feeling anxious because we can't identify any significant changes in our lives that could have occasioned such feelings. Although family and friends surround us, we feel disconnected. What once interested us no longer does. No matter how much we try losing ourselves by working or socializing, we are painfully self-conscious of our inability to do so.

As disconcerting and painful as these times might be, our isolation is often self-imposed. For example, our discomfort may arise from our own ambivalence about intimacy. We are uneasy about being too distant or too close to others. While we anxiously wait for the doorbell or telephone to ring, when it does, we hesitate to answer. Waiting to be invited out, we are apprehensive when we are. Since connections help us establish our worth in others' eyes, when we feel so disconnected it might seem we have no special identity. Uncertain about what is happening, we find it difficult if not impossible to explain why we are distressed. Since relatives, friends, and coworkers might wonder what is happening to us, their confusion reinforces our feeling of isolation. Carl Jung's concept of the persona as a source and sometimes the sole source of seeing ourselves through others eyes helps us understand why we experience confusion and uncertainty about our identity during the transition we are considering.

33

Persona Identity

We adapt to the world through the *persona*, a Latin word from which we derive the English words person and personality. According to Jung, the persona is how we present ourselves to others through our roles, our functions, and our status. We not only present ourselves as the doctor, business executive, teacher, husband, or mother, and so on, but we present ourselves in line with others' expectations of how these roles are to be played out. However nasty, angry, loving, or vengeful we might feel, we also feel obliged to behave according to norms prescribed by the various institutions and agencies within society.

Although there is a wide assortment of personae available, circumstances limit those we develop. We grow up, get married or remain single, have certain interests, and develop our talents along the lines consistent with the personae we have adopted. In this way over a period of years we build up a quasi-identity based on the personae we have assumed.

Our interactions with others are based on our personae. A person is a teacher, married, and the father of four. Another remains single, becomes a computer expert, and plays the piano. If these persons should meet, immediately after introductions they might ask, "What do you do?" Why this question? Because as soon as each knows what the other does each now has some idea how to interact. But even when they speak about their personal lives they are relating through the persona, e.g., one is married and a father while the other is single. "We are what we do" is a brief definition of a persona identity.

There is nothing wrong in identifying ourselves through these personae provided we're aware that we are not merely any one or any combination of personae. There is more to the person than being a banker or the father of a family. However, as time passes, there is a tendency to see ourselves solely in terms of our roles and how people expect us to live out these roles. Practically speaking our quasi-identity *is* our identity. While there's still potential to develop, the more we channel our energies through the same personae, the more we limit creative development in other directions.

It is obvious how uncomfortable we would be wearing the same size trousers or dress from age ten to thirty. Yet it's amazing how we restrict the growth of our personalities by channeling who we are through limited and limiting personae for many years.

During a transition, or desert experience, the limitations of our quasi-identity become apparent, as we grow increasingly restless over the limitations it imposes. We can no longer summon up the energies to channel through these personae, and we feel disconnected from the ways our energies had been invested for so long. This whole process is a dimension of "disidentification" in which we are psychologically stripped of the familiar personae by means of which we have seen ourselves, been seen by others, and achieved our identity among them.

Although painful, desert experiences provide opportunities to gain insight into who we are apart from the persona through which we and/or others have seen us. For example someone who is involved in work to the exclusion of everything else might find the desert experience an occasion to reflect on his priorities. He now has the opportunity to disengage from the persona of the workaholic. Of course, this might be distressing because his work has colored his understanding of who he is.

The disconnection we experience during the liminal or desert period in a transition seems to be nature's way of disengaging us from habitual, sometimes compulsive ways of relating through our personae. It is then possible for us to commit ourselves freely to new projects and relationships, or to recommit ourselves to present ones with a clearer appreciation of what our commitment does or doesn't entail. So the workaholic might realize that while work is important there is more to life than his work.

It is unfortunate that today those who desire a deeper understanding of themselves in their relationship with others, the cosmos, and God seldom find anyone to guide them through their desert experiences. This is why journey stories from our religious traditions are so helpful. They assist us to gain insight into our experiences. Here we consider Jesus' own desert experience and what we might learn from it as we struggle to make sense out of the desert experiences of our transitions.

Jesus' Baptism

Jesus' temptations are a dramatic foreshadowing of his impending confrontations throughout his public ministry. This encounter with Satan highlights whom Jesus' adversaries were in his ministry, those calling into question, misinterpreting, or deliberately distorting what he understood himself and his mission to be.

By understanding this biblical scene as a composite of several confrontations with friends and enemies alike, we are free to explore how Jesus might have experienced these conflicts during the three years of his ministry. In other words, he might have had several "desert experiences" rather than simply the one presented in the gospel. As Raymond Brown has pointed out:

> *Scenes in John show clearly that the three "temptations" or testings (gaining kingly power, working a bread-miracle for the wrong purpose, showing off greatness in Jerusalem), dramatized in Matthew and Luke as a direct conflict between Jesus and the devil or Satan, had a counterpart in Jesus' ministry.*[1]

The counterpart to which he refers can be seen in John 6:15 in which the crowd reacts to the multiplication of the loaves by trying to make Jesus an earthly king, in John 6:26-27 where they can get more easily obtained bread, and in John 7:1-9 where Jesus' brothers want him to leave Galilee in order to show himself off to the world in Judea. Brown's comments clearly identify the temptations or "testings." They are appeals to Jesus, suggesting how he might profitably see himself through the eyes of his disciples, relatives, and crowds.

Before considering how Jesus' temptations occurred in his public ministry, it is important to consider his baptismal experience in which he hears the voice from heaven say, "You are my Son, the Beloved; with you I am well pleased" (Luke 3:22). The baptismal experience is significant to the extent that it enables us to see the temptations during his ministry as appeals from others to live his life for the wrong reasons, as Brown suggests.

No one is certain whether Jesus' awareness of a special intimacy with God occurred over a period of time or at the moment of his baptism. John Meier writes that, most likely, Jesus developed the key insights into his relationship with God as Father, and the activity of the Spirit in his life over a period of time extending from his leaving home through leaving the company of John the Baptist. However, at the very least, Jesus' baptism "meant a fundamental break in his life; baptism as watershed. As far as our meager sources allow us to know, before his baptism by John, Jesus was a respectable, unexceptional, and unnoticed woodworker."[2] We might interpret this gradual development of key insights into his relationship over a period of time as contributing to the development of his persona identity. Meier's observations conform to what we know about many conversion experiences. Often a dramatic event is preceded by a process of change and followed by a period in which the person struggles to discern the best way of living out the conversion experience. Meier's description of Jesus as an unexceptional and unnoticed woodworker is a remarkable contrast with the words Jesus heard at his baptism, "You are my Son, the Beloved; with you I am well pleased." Here, Jesus experienced a revelation of God's overwhelming love for him.

To appreciate how Jesus' baptism affected him, we might recall situations where we felt as if the sun had shone on us in a special way. Falling in love, or being desired and noticed in a special way bears some resemblance to Jesus' experience. It need not necessarily be one incident or one person that generates this feeling of being favored. We could see ourselves as special because of a whole series of events, which confirm us in the career, or profession on which we had embarked. Expressions like "being on cloud nine" or "being on top of the world" convey the sense of being favored by a person, an event, or sequence of events, e.g., artistic, athletic, academic. Sometimes we aren't even certain who or what favors us. "Someone," we say, "is looking after us." These different ways in which we feel special might not be as intense as Jesus' baptismal experience but they are intimations or "rumors of transcendence."[3]

Jesus' experience of being God's beloved is a privileged experience, but it isn't an unmixed blessing. Feeling special carries with it the possibility of inflation. This means that one gets a big head or is puffed up. Initially, people who fall in love are in love with love. They feel there are no limits to their love for one another. In the whole world no one else loves or could love as they do. The emphasis is on how they see themselves through the eyes of the beloved. If a person feels blessed and singled out in some artistic or athletic achievement, he or she might get carried away, and completely ignore other needs (bodily, emotional) in the pursuit of greater achievements that further enhance their reputation in others' eyes.

If we see ourselves as specially blessed because we are citizens of this or that country, then we could easily become arrogant toward citizens of other countries. Likewise, we might show this attitude toward other religious traditions. God has blessed us with the truth. Others are simply misguided.

Given Jesus' experience of being God's beloved, could he have been tempted to misinterpret its meaning? And if so, what form or shape might the temptation have taken? Would it have been a passing thought or recurred during key transitions in his ministry as Raymond Brown suggested? And did his mission become clearer to him because of these temptations?

Miracle Worker

The devil said to him, "If you are the Son of God, command this stone to become a loaf of bread." Jesus answered him, "It is written, 'One does not live by bread alone.' " — Luke 4:3-4

"If ..." If you are really special then you'll have to prove it by being the miracle worker. The devil equates being God's beloved with the persona of a miracle worker. All Jesus has to do to prove that he is God's beloved is to perform a simple miracle, turn a stone into a loaf of bread.

We can appreciate the strength of the appeal. We often think our worth is dependent on how we perform or on what we deliver. The more we do the more we read how special we are in others' eyes. The play's the thing! Some people live their lives for display purposes only. We laugh at politicians anxious over their standing in the polls, or ambitious clerics intent on pleasing the hierarchy. Surely we've also felt the need to prove ourselves by saying and doing what we think might gain others' approval.

"If you are God's favorite...." But Jesus says, "It is written, 'One does not live by bread alone.' " The devil fails to persuade Jesus that he could prove he's special by being the wonder worker, and there is every indication that during his ministry Jesus resisted similar suggestions from others.

Raymond Brown says as much when he explains why Jesus makes a hasty departure after he multiplied the loaves (John 6:15). Impressed by his physical miracle, the crowd was about to make Jesus king by force. He refused to give them more bread to prove that he was a second Moses.[4]

If Jesus did anything in his ministry that might have tempted him to think he was special, it was his healing miracles. To be admired for mending minds and bodies is heady stuff! Why not capitalize on it? Surely others would agree that Jesus was very special because of his healing powers!

Dominic Crossan observes that Jesus' family certainly was aware how special Jesus was because of his healing powers. It would have made sense to them for Jesus to settle down in his hometown of Nazareth and set up a healing cult. In this way he could have been the patron, his family the brokers, and the sick who came to Jesus, his clients to be healed. This would have benefited everyone.

> But instead Jesus kept to the road, brought healing to those who needed it, and had, as it were, to start off anew every day. That was no way to run a healing ministry and no way to treat your family, especially within the world of Mediterranean values.[5]

Crossan believes that Jesus' idea was to heal people who in turn would become healers. It was not his intent to be The Healer to whom everybody would journey to be healed. But Jesus does not yield to the temptation to become identified with his wonder-working abilities nor does he feel the need to prove himself special through his miracles.

Man Of Power

Then the devil led him up and showed him in an instant all the kingdoms of the world. And the devil said to him, "To you I will give their glory and all their authority; for it has been given over to me, and I give it to anyone I please. If you, then, will worship me, it will all be yours." Jesus answered him, "It is written, 'Worship the Lord your God, and serve only him.' " — Luke 4:5-8

The devil's appeal to Jesus to prove himself God's beloved through performing miracles is also a covert appeal to Jesus' possible predilection for power. This appeal is explicit in the second temptation. While none of us have ever been tempted by the prospect of so much power, we ought not to be blind to the countless ways in which we might abuse power in order to see ourselves as powerful in others' eyes.

There are the obvious ways: gun the engine; give orders from a big desk; tell people over a loudspeaker to quiet down; write letters dictating how people are to live their lives; yell at them; hold a gun to their heads; threaten them with the loss of their souls. We exercise power by threatening, cajoling, withholding or dispensing favors, being sexually or emotionally abusive. We can also wield power in more covert ways. We can control others through silent power like passive aggressive pouting when we want our way, or through evaluation forms that determine another's future. Often in our protests about being helpless we can get others to do our bidding. We abdicate responsibility by putting power in others' hands and then accuse them of mismanaging our lives. How skillfully we manage others to make them look manipulative!

Power also resides in what we possess. Prize possessions! There's no need to itemize all the things and people we call our own that can make us feel special. The truth is that it doesn't take much. "I need a baby to love me ... to let me know that I am somebody!" Whatever is my or mine or ours can be the source of feeling powerful. It doesn't matter what is mine, so long as it is mine.

As we have seen, the crowds would have forced Jesus to be king after they had watched him miraculously multiply the bread. But he made a hasty departure because he would have nothing to do with kingdoms of this world. The same situation arose again in John's account of the triumphal entry into Jerusalem. When the crowd goes out with palm branches to hail the King of Israel, Jesus finds a young ass to ride upon. In doing so he negates how the crowd chooses to see him. His action is designed to remind the people of Zechariah's promise (9:9) that the king was to be primarily a king of peace and salvation, rather than one of political power. It is possible to imagine Jesus gently mocking authority and power as most of us see power. Not a legionnaire's horse, but a donkey. In other words, instead of coming in on an army tank he chose to enter Jerusalem on a coaster wagon. Can you imagine someone pulling the pope into town in a wagon? Or asking the President to ride on the front of a bicycle-built-for-two with the First Lady on the back? Jesus didn't seem to think a big horse, the equivalent to a bullet-proof limo, suited him. He was satisfied with a donkey.

Recall, also, that on one occasion when Jesus' disciples were arguing among themselves who was the greatest, Jesus told them that his associates had to be people who didn't insist on being at the top of the heap. He wasn't impressed with people who threw their weight around, especially if it was to demean others. There was enough of that kind already in circulation! What he preferred were persons who used power to empower others. He was interested in helping people recognize they had the power to effect changes in their lives. He wasn't interested in putting on the glad rags of power to impress others. He resisted the temptation to prove himself special through the use of power.

Desert experiences, then, are occasions of grace when we are disengaged from our routine ways of being and doing, and can begin to see destructive patterns of behavior we have been pursuing. But seeing through our power ploys doesn't automatically mean relinquishing them. Power is a source of identity, a mirror showing us why we think, and why we think others think we're special.

The Invulnerable One

> *Then the devil took him to Jerusalem, and placed him on the pinnacle of the temple, saying to him, "If you are the Son of God, throw yourself down from here, for it is written, 'He will command his angels concerning you, to protect you,' and 'On their hands they will bear you up, so that you will not dash your foot against a stone.'" Jesus answered him, "It is said, 'Do not put the Lord your God to the test.'"*   — Luke 3:9-12

"If you are the beloved, then God will be there to protect you. You won't suffer any letdowns. There'll be no disillusionment in your life. How could anyone who thinks you're special possibly leave you in your moment of need? So jump!"

It isn't always clear what triggers desert experiences, but some form of disillusionment is frequently associated with the experience. Sometimes the particular kind of disillusionment is obvious, sometimes not. Two people marry. They have high expectations of one another. Neither is able to live up to them. Disillusionment follows and unless the spouses rethink their expectations they'll be on their way to the divorce court. Or, someone gives his soul to a company for 25 years and then is told, "Sorry, you're no longer needed! Good-bye!" That's disillusioning and easily precipitates a desert experience. Or someone believes God is at his side through thick and thin. Then one day the doctor tells him his wife has lung cancer. He prays that God will heal her. She gets sicker. He prays intensely. She dies. Where has God been in all of this? On vacation? Disillusionment sets in. Not only does he wonder if God has left the scene, but if there is a God at all. This is clearly a desert experience.

But in some desert experiences the source of disillusionment isn't so evident. For example, a mid-life crisis is not necessarily about any one incident or person who is the source of disillusionment. Life in general seems to be disillusioning. "Is this all there is? Has it all come to this?"

The reason for disillusionment in any desert experience lies in the illusion or the setup. The fiancé seemed to be the ideal conversationalist; but now the husband turns out to be too talkative. Or the worker assumes that the company has as much invested in him as he does in the company, and then one day he is abruptly given his walking papers. The illusions we have about how spouses, children, relatives, politicians, clergy, God, and so on, are expected to behave are too numerous to mention. One thing is certain. We never expect to be disillusioned! What we expect is that others be everything we had imagined them to be, and also that they see us as we needed them to see us! Not infrequently we might have expected the others to be God for us or us for them. We didn't realize it at the time but we were setting ourselves up to be more than we, or they, could ever be. We place others on pedestals and deify our ideologies. We even demand that God be God, as we need God to be. Yet, when our idols crumble we don't understand why they have let us down. The world is filled with revelations of the sacred but we have fixated on this or that revelation as if *it* were the sacred. We have created idols out of what originally might have been gifts from God.

Desert experiences are disillusioning but they can also liberate us from the many ways our illusions hold us hostage. The desert reveals how much energy we have invested in our illusions. Often, we have no time for anyone or anything other than our illusions about others or ourselves. Consider addictions! Addictions are forms of illusionment. The bottle, the job, the infatuation, the food binge, gambling — they all consume our energies so that we become hooked on them. Our desert experiences are times for withdrawal, for seeing through illusions and discovering how what had charmed and captivated our souls had also enslaved them.

"If you are God's beloved, God will not let you down." In the Gospel of Luke this is Jesus' last temptation. It is so seductive!

Surely if Jesus is special, no harm will come to him. But if it does? What then? We know he suffered his share of betrayals — from Judas and Peter, and other friends scurrying off to protect themselves from sharing Jesus' fate. Aware as he was of his disciples' weaknesses it still must have been disillusioning to be delivered into his enemies' hands by one disciple, denied by another, and abandoned by the rest. Yes, Jesus knew what it was like to have his own expectations shattered by people close to him. These betrayals must have left him wondering if he could ever trust anyone — anyone but the one whom he called Father. If Jesus had yielded to the temptation that his being special meant he couldn't be hurt, then his life would have ended in disillusionment. Yet, he knew enough about the human heart not to be overwhelmed by his disciples' betrayal.

More importantly, it was another way in which God let it be known that being the beloved of God did not depend at all on Jesus having to prove that he was invulnerable. Being special had nothing to do with anything he did or had. It had everything to do with seeing himself through God's eyes. In God's eyes he was special, and that was enough.

Jesus' baptismal experience of being God's beloved initiated his ministry. However, he was tested through a lifetime of struggles during which he was called to proclaim what he experienced: We are all special in God's eyes. Each of us is God's beloved and nothing we did or could do merits being special in God's eyes. We spend so much time proving to ourselves and to one another that we are, or ought to be, loveable in others' eyes, but often we never quite believe we're loved. There is always room for uncertainty. Then we have another go at it and another. Endlessly we fall back on our roles hoping that through these personae we'll finally convince others to see us as loveable, and through their eyes we'll see ourselves as loveable. Desert experiences are those opportune times in our lives when we might finally realize in our hearts that we are special, and that it has nothing to do with what we do. It is how God sees us. That is all.

Exercises

1. Describe in your notebook the different ways in which you behaved to the different persons you met during the past 24 hours. For example, how did you behave toward your spouse, children, co-workers, friends, or strangers? Did you behave differently toward the same person at different times? Did you find yourself behaving in the same way toward everyone whom you met during the day? A couple of words describing each encounter are sufficient. Then consider whether or not any of these behavioral patterns appear frequently in your life. If so, does this tell you anything about at least one persona you wear?

2. After the group has been given sufficient time to write something about their patterns of behavior, take time for discussing how much time and energy is consumed wearing what might be the dominant persona, e.g., teacher, parent, etc. What are the strengths and weaknesses of channeling most of one's energies through a particular persona? For example, if someone channels energies primarily through the role or persona of the teacher is there room in the person's life for expressing these energies in other ways? Do certain professions lend themselves to channeling most energies through a particular persona, e.g., a doctor or clergyperson? Does the role of being Mom or Dad leave no room for other personae coming into play?

Questions For Discussion

1. Have you ever experienced the loss of a persona through divorce, or a family member's death, or retirement, or anything else, which gave you a sense of identity? If so, was this a desert experience for you as described in the chapter? Did you feel lost? Did you feel any loss of self-esteem? Depressed? Or did you feel that in spite of feeling lost this could also be a time of new possibilities, of potential for developing some aspect of yourself hitherto unexplored?

2. The period during which Jesus was tempted in the desert was a time of being tested. The tests described in the chapter are an appeal to consider himself special based on being the "miracle worker," then "a man of power," and finally "the invulnerable one." Have you ever been tempted in your desert experiences or other times to base your worth on any of these personae or others you can think of?

3. Were there support groups, e.g., family and friends, available to help you through your desert or liminal experiences? Did your faith in God help you? How important were these support groups for you? On the other hand, did you feel abandoned by God and alone in the desert? Or did you later realize that you might have been closer to God than ever during these times since you might have cried out to God, as you had never done before?

---

1. Raymond Brown, *An Introduction To The New Testament* (New York: Doubleday, 1997), p. 177.

2. John Meier, *A Marginal Jew*, Vol. 2 (New York: Doubleday, 1994), pp. 108, 109.

3. Peter L. Berger, *A Rumor Of Angels* (Garden City, New Jersey: Doubleday, 1969).

4. Raymond Brown, "Incidents That Are Units In The Synoptic Gospels But Dispersed In St. John" *Catholic Biblical Quarterly* Vol. XXIII, No. 2, April 1961, pp. 152-155.

5. Dominic Crossan, *Jesus: A Revolutionary Biography* (San Francisco: HarperCollins, 1994), p. 99.

Chapter 3

From Who's Out To Who's In

Objective: To become aware of how the purity system in Jesus' day is alive in our insider mentality today.

> *In those days when there was again a great crowd without anything to eat, he called his disciples and said to them, "I have compassion for the crowd, because they have been with me now for three days and have nothing to eat. If I send them away hungry to their homes, they will faint on the way — and some of them have come from a great distance." His disciples replied, "How can one feed these people with bread here in the desert?" He asked them, "How many loaves do you have?"*
>
> *They said, "Seven." Then he ordered the crowd to sit down on the ground; and he took the seven loaves, and after giving thanks he broke them and gave them to his disciples to distribute; and they distributed them to the crowd. They had also a few small fish; and after blessing them, he ordered that these too should be distributed. They ate and were filled; and they took up the broken pieces left over, seven baskets full. Now there were about four thousand people. And he sent them away.*   — Mark 8:1-10

In the last chapter we saw how Jesus discovered in the desert that being loved by God didn't depend on personal achievements or titles. God's love alone made him special. Often in our transitions we, too, discover that what we thought made us special *isn't* necessarily so. We become painfully aware that everything we had regarded as important is relatively insignificant, and if we are fortunate we gain the insight that what really matters is that we and everyone else are special because we are loved in God's eyes.

It is one thing to achieve the insight that being special means being loved in God's eyes. But it is another to figure out how we are to share this knowledge with others. All of us are loved in God's eyes, but many of us might feel these are empty words if we are treated as second-class citizens, e.g., the divorced and remarried, gays and lesbians, persons of color, and the underclass in our society. Crossing or blurring boundaries can have repercussions, as those who have been punished by ecclesial or civic authorities have discovered.

Social, political, and religious structures largely define our relationships with one another. Although important for maintaining order, if structural considerations become the overriding concern, they clash with Jesus' fundamental insight, namely, we are all loved in God's eyes. Then we need to be reminded of Jesus' program through which he began to incarnate his revolutionary vision that none of us is to be excluded from God's love nor treated as second-class citizens under God's rule. In other words in his preaching, healing, and eating with others, he changed the norms of his society. He redefined who was an insider and who was an outsider, who was in and who was out. This was no small task in a society that appears to have been segregated into the nobodies and the somebodies, the losers and the winners.

In this journey story Jesus travels to a deserted place. There he challenges his society in order to transform it in accordance with his vision. Along the way we shall see the challenge it presents to us as we attempt to implement his vision of seeing all people through God's eyes.

The focus of many commentaries, sermons, and reflections on this journey story has been Jesus' multiplication of the loaves and fishes. While this miracle undoubtedly merits attention, emphasis on it has overshadowed something equally important, namely the place where the miracle takes place and the nature of the crowd with whom Jesus ate.

Unlike the previous temptation story, here Jesus is not alone in the desert. Mark writes that 4,000 people were with him. Even if Mark exaggerates the number of persons present, we can still imagine a sizeable crowd present for three days. Most likely they had traveled from different villages. Just as likely, many, if not most, of them didn't know one another personally, nor did they know one another's occupation.

Since it was uninhabited, the desert was considered to be a place of chaos by the Jews. Those who journeyed there were no longer in a space or time considered civilized or holy. This is the kind of space we could refer to as "liminal" or in-between space. Whatever might divide and distinguish people in a structured society did not obtain in unstructured, chaotic space. The significance of this space where Jesus feeds the multitude will shortly become apparent.

Since the crowd had already been there for three days they had nothing to sustain them as they congregated in Jesus' presence. We can assume this must have been a significant time for them. If we think of gatherings like the demonstrations around the world against war in Iraq we might get a sense of the fellowship generated among those who gathered.

But it is also possible that we who live in a free, democratic society take for granted gathering as equals, and therefore might not be terribly impressed by what occurred in the desert. Yet what happened there and throughout Jesus' ministry was more than a community of equals sharing fellowship. Jesus' eating with others there and elsewhere not only generated fellowship, but it was also an indirect attack on the purity system as interpreted by the religious leadership. Here it is worth noting:

> Since the areas outside towns and villages were considered places of chaos, meals did not normally take place there. People did not picnic in the first-century Mediterranean. Proper care could not be taken in the preparation of food or the other necessities of ritual purity.[1]

Some explanation of this system will aid us in seeing the religious and political significance of Jesus' action. It will also help us comprehend how Jesus' action is no less startling today than it was 2,000 years ago.

The Purity System

There is an expression that is intended to bridge the often stormy relationship between psychology and religion: "holiness is wholeness." It means that complete, healthy human beings are also holy human beings. There is no opposition between being holy and being whole. Psychology and religion need not be enemies. They can be allies. Justification for this insight can be found in the Bible. In Leviticus we read, "Ye shall be holy, for I the Lord your God am holy" (Leviticus 19:2). Since God is complete or whole, it followed that if the Jews were to be holy as God is holy, then they too had to be complete or whole. To be whole was to be pleasing to God. With an honorable history rooted in scriptures why should anyone feel uneasy about the holiness — wholeness equation?

In Jesus' time this core value of being holy as God is holy was in danger of becoming the *exclusive* value among the influential religious elite in the Jewish community. These were the powerful Jerusalem aristocrats whose opinion mattered when it came to identifying who was whole or unwhole, holy or unholy. In the highly stratified society of first-century Israel, it was this powerful aristocracy's opinion that counted. Of course, there were also those unfortunate people who didn't need to worry about losing their integrity because they had already been identified as flawed from the day they were born! Among them were the lame, the blind, the deaf, bastards, eunuchs, and others physically impaired.

But even those who were considered whole had reason to be uneasy. They could lose their integrity either by not defending their bodily orifices from contaminants leaving or entering, or by not monitoring contact with defective persons, places, or things. The endangered list included menstruating women, men having seminal emissions, or persons exchanging bodily fluids with others considered ritually unclean. Even a kiss, or a hug, or a touch could be defiling as could consorting with or working for the Romans.

In this atmosphere Jesus openly invited others to eat with him. From the elite's perspective even eating with unclean persons was contaminating. Think how Jesus' sharing food with the crowd in the desert must have offended the guardians of holiness. Eating with so many unknowns in the middle of some godforsaken place! Nothing like blurring differences between the clean and the unclean. It didn't matter to the aristocrats that the people whom Jesus fed left with full hearts and bellies. This was irrelevant to those who zealously pursued holiness.

Every time Jesus ate indiscriminately with others he violated the purity code because he ate with whomever he pleased. He was not acting like some anarchist who wanted to destroy the purity system. Writing about Mark's Gospel, Jerome Neyrey insists that it would be erroneous to say that Mark repudiates the purity system solely because he presents Jesus disregarding or contesting certain purity rules. Mark "portrays Jesus according to a reformed idea of purity, in which lines are being redrawn and boundaries loosened."[2] The core value of the Jewish system was God's "holiness" but Jesus emphasizes "mercy." While God's holiness was symbolized in God's act of creation, God's mercy was symbolized in God's free election and God's unpredictable gift of covenant grace. Jesus was concerned about being hospitable and inclusive, and this was based on mercy as the primary value. The religious elite's emphasis on holiness resulted in an exclusivism.[3]

Jesus' attempt to redraw the lines of the purity system can also be seen in his debate with certain Pharisees on the kinds of food which could or could not be eaten (Mark 7:1-22). Some Pharisees objected to his apparent lack of concern about not eating properly prepared food. They were angry that Jesus minimized the importance of safeguarding bodily boundaries through contacting anything unclean. But Jesus had not denied what they valued. His actions simply drew attention to the importance of mercy, which they had neglected in their zeal to promote holiness. He told his disciples that what mattered was what came out of a person's heart and not what entered the body, as some Pharisees had emphasized.

The religious elite would have labeled Jesus impure because he was constantly crossing boundaries and reaching out to those considered impure. Yet, when Jesus crossed boundaries he didn't become impure. Those whom he touched became pure. Through his open table fellowship and his healing actions, those who felt alienated could feel that they belonged.

In view of what has been said about Jesus reaching out to the crowd in the desert, what he did was more than an act of kindness. At the very least it was an act of solidarity by standing alongside the marginalized of his society. Eating with them symbolized his refusal to acknowledge the rules for determining who was clean and who was unclean, who was out and who was in. In this he risked incurring the wrath of the elite and being accused of having no honor. Given the importance of honor and shame in his society, disgrace would have been a terrible price to pay.

Open Commensality

Jesus repeatedly risked offending the powerful religious elite whenever he sat down to eat with others. His table fellowship was not only a social event, it was also a religious and political event. Dominic Crossan speaks of Jesus' table fellowship as "open commensality." By this he means that Jesus' disregard for maintaining clear distinctions between people, based on the highly stratified society in which he lived, also symbolized his understanding of what was and was not essential under the reign of God:

> *The Kingdom of God as a process of open commensality, of a nondiscriminating table depicting in miniature a non-discriminating society, clashes fundamentally with honor and shame, those basic values of ancient Mediterranean culture.[4]*

> *Open commensality is the symbol and embodiment of radical egalitarianism, of an absolute equality of people that denies the validity of any discrimination between them and negates the necessity of any hierarchy among them.[5]*

But what does all this have to do with us? What might we learn from Jesus' sojourn in the desert? What does his attempts to reform the purity system mean for us? What would following Jesus' practice of open commensality mean today?

Striving For Holiness Today

Here we need to take a second look at the holiness-wholeness equation. In a secular society such as ours, the struggle many have with being well-adjusted and acceptable to others might seem unconnected with being holy. Yet, the religious fervor with which people seek to be whole psychologically and/or physically reveals a yearning to be found acceptable that can only be described as religious.

Consider Molly O'Neill's observations in her article "The Morality of Fat" in which she writes that our country's love affair with healthful eating has become a national religion. Our preoccupation with fat has become a struggle between the good of rational restraint and the evil of base human instinct. We have a low-fat theology in which dietary prudence is equivalent to virtue while our taste for fat is immoral. She refers to Sidney Mintz (then professor of anthropology at Johns Hopkins University) who maintains there are strong moral overtures to Americans' eating habits. Our lively appreciation of sin manifest in eating behaviors colored by this appreciation.

Moreover, the amount of fat we eat and the form in which we eat it signifies status. Persons aware of the latest nutritional and medical research are mostly affluent urbanites. Statistically, the more affluent and educated, the more likely they are to buy raw ingredients. It costs more to cook healthfully, and it requires a certain knowledge and expertise. Quoting the food historian Margaret Visser, low-fat cooking is a "conspicuous display of competence." In contrast are the consumers who purchase processed low-fat food. These folks have:

> *simpler, low-fat faith — an unquestioning belief in technology and advertising. Regarding the four bags of reduced-fat corn chips he was about to buy, one overweight shopper said plaintively, "Make me thin!"*[6]

Just as the followers of John Harvey Kellogg who lived in the nineteenth century (well-known as a doctor who was a vegetarian and who had an obsession with the bowels and their elimination):

were unshakable in their belief in spiritual redemption through clean bowels, today's low-fat society is convinced that salvation is to be found in plaque-free arterial walls.[7]

While O'Neill doesn't use terms like whole and unwhole, holy or unholy, we can conclude from her remarks that depending on the food we eat some of us are "wholier" than others! Our religious concerns surface even more sharply in the extremes to which people go to become acceptable or better than others. For example, Vanessa Grigoriadis writing a *New York Times* article, 'Rest The Tummy, Restore the Soul," points to a more recent trend toward fasting. The purpose in fasting is to detoxify the polluted body:

These new believers have joined a fasting corps formerly made up of the devoutly religious, raw-foodists and the chronically ill.[8]

She quotes one psychologist who equates the mindset of these zealous fasters with anorexics.

There is a sense of satisfaction in fasting. The idea that you can overcome or transcend your bodily urges, your needs, and the environmental stimuli of food conveys a sense of purity, righteousness and virtue.[9]

This sounds familiar if we recall Jesus words in Matthew 6:16, "And whenever you fast, do not look dismal, like the hypocrites, for they disfigure their faces so as to show others that they are fasting." She quotes yet another psychologist who maintains:

that the current fasters may be reacting to how unhealthy our society is about food, who are fearful of the impact of fast foods and the increase in obesity. So the segment of the upper middle class who have time to do something like fasting will do it.[10]

So people who are anorexic or bulimic in their own way are as religiously concerned about eating "clean" food as were many of the people in Jesus' time. Anorexics are appalled at the thought of eating anything that might render them unclean and therefore unacceptable. On the other hand bulimics gorge themselves on anything and everything only to cleanse themselves later of what had defiled and made them unacceptable. These disorders signal a larger problem — our culture's misguided priority on what makes a person, especially a woman, whole and acceptable, namely, a slim, youthful appearance. Along these lines we might also mention the cult of the body at the workout, diet, and cosmetic surgery centers of worship where we spend millions of dollars annually.

Those who aren't too concerned about eating habits may still display anxiety about bodily integrity and purity in their purchases of those guardians of the bodies' portals which we call deodorants, scented soaps, perfumes, colognes, shave lotions, and toothpastes. We even ritually clean our toilets with Tidy Bowl and Sani-Flush.

But purity concerns are also present in the church as we judge who's in or out, whole or unwhole, and what the punishment ought to be for those judged unclean. A number of years ago when Jacqueline Kennedy Onassis died and it was announced that the Mass of Christian Burial was to be held at Saint Ignatius Loyola Church in New York, a number of people called into the parish and were less than kind. Father Modry, the pastor, composed a brief essay for the parish bulletin to address their complaints. In it he pointed out:

> *Many people are buried from the Church: divorced people, homosexuals, daily communicants, married people who may have been unfaithful, parents who were less than generous to their children, fallen away Catholics, "death bed" converts, embittered old people. We are all brought into this church so that our relatives and friends can gather around the table of the Lord to pray for us and entrust us to the infinite mercy of God.*
>
> *This is a shocking thought to those who find it hard to believe that the church can be so bold as to recommend to the Lord's mercy people whose faults may be apparent or who lived their lives as less than saints. The shock is a good one to experience because it is one that fills every page of the Gospel story.*[11]

Of course there were also a number of persons who were upset that Senator Ted Kennedy received communion at the Mass. Since he was remarried they wondered what right he had to receive communion! Unfortunately the word about Jesus' open table fellowship hasn't gotten out to those responsible for restating the ban on the divorced and remarried receiving communion several years later. Clearly these remarried people are out! Charles Davis states it well when he writes:

> The Catechism of the Catholic Church (2384 and 1650) states: "A Catholic who remarries without an annulment is in a situation of public and permanent adultery" and is officially denied communion. Yet 1651 instructs priests to "manifest an attentive solicitude, so that they (the remarried) do not consider themselves separated from the Church." Does it make sense to deny us communion but also say we are not to consider ourselves separated from the church?[12]

Davis is not alone in his call for the divorced and remarried being able to receive communion. In a survey conducted as far back as 1992, 72 percent of the Catholics said divorced and remarried Catholics should be allowed to receive communion.[13]

Even bishops can expect to be out if they're not careful. Some years ago Bishop Jacques Gaillot, the French bishop of Evreux, was removed from his See because he crossed the boundaries. He had been vocal in urging a married priesthood, defending homosexuals, etc. What must have been the beginning of the end for him was coming out in support of a proposed French law to recognize same sex unions, and once having recited a prayer of "welcome" for a gay couple. In a French publication he explained that he had received a request from a gay couple to bless their marriage, "Please receive us, although we are pariahs of the church. I've got AIDS. My life will soon come to an end. Therefore we would very much like you to bless our union. It would be such a comfort." Gaillot said he agreed to meet the couple and "to say a prayer, as a sign of welcome and understanding." Crossing the boundary to embrace a couple on the outs put Gaillot out. He was fired from his position![14]

Several years ago a friend of mine was ordained to the permanent diaconate. When I arrived at the cathedral with some of my Protestant friends, I sat in my pew and began reading the lengthy notes in the program about the conditions the congregants had to meet if they wished to receive communion. They were nothing extraordinary, but I was struck by the fact that they were so boldly spelled out lest someone in the congregation should fail to recognize them and go astray. The guests had come to celebrate another banquet with Jesus and conditions had been laid down about who was out and who was in, who could or couldn't fully celebrate. Reading the notes was like reading a menu and being told that some of the table companions had better plan on dieting because the entrée wasn't for them.

What did the notes say? For our Protestant brothers and sisters: If any of them had thought of receiving communion at the table, the directive was clear — sorry, but they couldn't. They were out! For those who were clean all over was the reminder that if they had drunk any liquids within an hour prior to communion then they'd have to forget communion! They could come back at another time. Conditions for approaching the Lord's festive table had been clearly set forth. The defense line was in place. Anybody who thought, "I have this carte blanche, no-strings-attached-invitation to dine with Jesus" had another thought coming. So much for open table fellowship!

As I sat there I tried to imagine Jesus demanding certain conditions be met before sharing bread with those hungry men and women 2,000 years ago in the desert. Would he have carefully screened and scrutinized the crowd as he preached? Would he have said, "I need to know if you folks share my belief system? Do we see eye to eye on matters? Are we all singing the same tune? Or is there someone out there who's off key? Are some of you heterodox? And if there are some folks who don't share my beliefs with *i*s dotted and *t*s crossed, would you do me a favor? No matter how hungry you are keep your hands off the bread and fish when they're passed your way. They're not for you!"

Or would Jesus have pursed his lips, shaken a finger and railed, "Look, I know that some of you men have been fooling around and

I have proof positive that we have some shady ladies basking in this sun! I'm telling you and everybody else who's been up to no good — unless you've cleaned up your act, you can sit by yourself because you aren't getting anything I have to give!"

Yes, I tried to imagine Jesus laying down conditions. But given what I know about Jesus: his attempts at redrawing the lines of the purity system in favor of mercy and compassion; his inclusive rather than his exclusive approach to others; and his open table fellowship throughout his ministry, I could not imagine him setting such conditions then nor now.

It might also be objected that this form of open fellowship will create chaos. Aren't we fostering promiscuity or a do-as-you-damn-well please attitude by not being more concerned about who's in and who's out? Again Crossan's comments on open commensality are helpful. Commenting on a parable found in Matthew 22:9-10 and Luke 14:21b-23 in which a person throwing a party asks his servants to go out and invite whomever they can find, he says Jesus lived out his own parable since he didn't make the appropriate distinctions and discriminations required of table fellowship. No wonder he was accused of being a glutton, a drunkard, and a friend of tax collectors, whores, and sinners:

> All of those terms—tax collectors, sinners, whores—
> are in this case derogatory terms for those with whom,
> in the opinion of the name callers, open and free asso-
> ciation should be avoided.[15]

Furthermore, at least one biblical scholar, E.P. Sanders, observes that unlike John who preached a baptism of repentance followed by restitution, followed by acceptance, Jesus made no such demands. And this was both the novelty and offense of Jesus' message. Association with Jesus was not dependent on conversion to the law. Jesus offered fellowship to Israel's wicked as a sign that God would save them:

> The wicked who heeded him would be included in the
> kingdom even though they did not repent as it was uni-
> versally understood — that is, even though they did not

make restitution, sacrifice, and turn to obedience to the
law.[16]

While John's message was a conditioned acceptance, Jesus' message was unconditioned. He didn't pass out meal tickets with conversion as the price of admission. Sanders argues that if Jesus had demanded conversion of those who accepted his invitation to table fellowship then how would Jesus have been any different from the religious establishment which also accepted sinners after conversion? There would have been no difference at all, and therefore no reason for being upset with Jesus. But those who opposed Jesus called him a drunkard because he hung around with known sinners and accepted them into his community unconditionally. It was this that made Jesus' table fellowship a dangerous activity.

Whether we accept or reject Sanders' or Crossan's interpretations about table fellowship, we cannot escape the fact that over and over Jesus crossed boundaries and rendered himself impure according to the prevailing understanding of the purity system. Certainly his table fellowship illustrated crossing boundaries regardless of the dispositions of those whom he invited to eat with him. That he was accused of encouraging a do-as-you-damn-well-please attitude is obvious. Encouraging others toward open commensality today invites a similar accusation. It follows then that some people could get into trouble acting as Jesus did.

The miraculous multiplication of loaves is significant not simply because Jesus was able to do more with less but because of how he shared that food with others so profligately. It is significant both because he invited *everybody* to eat with him and because in doing this he modeled the attitude that we ought to embody in our table fellowship.

It is also a reminder that anytime we become preoccupied with clearly defining who's in and who's out or who belongs and who doesn't, we might be celebrating some kind of fellowship but it is not Jesus' fellowship. Nor should we think that it is enough to say that we have enjoyed mutuality during our fellowship. For open commensality is also meant to be a challenge to be inclusive rather than exclusive in society as well as at our rituals within the church. Nothing less will do.

Exercises

1. Write a paragraph or two on an occasion when you felt like an outsider, e.g., at a party or at a gathering with others of a different race, gender, religion, etc. Ask yourself if you were made to feel inferior or different? If so, how were you made to feel this way?

    Describe in the same exercise when you felt like an insider, e.g., when along with others you thought of an other or others as outsiders who were present at a gathering. Describe how you felt later when you thought of your own behavior as a contributing factor to someone feeling like an outsider? If the person regarded as an outsider was a parent or friend did you feel ashamed of that person? Still later did you feel ashamed of yourself because of your earlier feelings? Have your experiences of being an insider or outsider had an effect on your behavior?

2. Write a paragraph or two about a time when you attempted to break down the barrier between outsiders and insiders. Did you encounter hostility or resistance? Were you surprised by some breakthrough that helped both persons or groups come together?

Questions For Discussion

1. Whom do we, our families, or our churches organizations treat as outsiders and insiders? What is there about us that lead us to see some people as outsiders and some as insiders? Race? Religion? Sexual orientation? Gender? Income? Education?

2. The answer to whom we identify as outsiders and insiders leads to the next question. Are outsiders necessary for insiders because insiders define themselves not by who they are but by who they are not? Is there fear that if those who are different become insiders, then those already insiders will feel they are

losing what is unique and special about themselves? Do insiders fear that their being an insider will cease to exist in any definable way should the boundaries between outsiders and insidres become blurred? Do you see the insider-outsider mentality present in religious traditions today? What kind of response did Jesus consistently give in word and deed to the insider-outsider, clean-unclean mentality of his day?

1. Bruce J. Malina and Richard L. Rohrbaugh *Social-Science Commentary on the Synoptic Gospels* (Minneapolis: Fortress Press, 1992), p. 217.

2. Jerome Neyrey (123) "Idea Of Purity In Mark's Gospel" *Semeia 35* (Decatur, Georgia: Scholars Press, 1986), pp. 91-1286. Neyrey, p. 9.

3. *Ibid.*, p. 9.

4. Dominic Crossan, *Jesus: A Revolutionary Biography* (San Francisco: Harper-Collins, 1994), p. 79.

5. *Ibid.*, p. 71.

6. Molly O'Neill, "The Morality Of Fat," *The New York Times* Magazine, March 10, 1996, pp. 37-39.

7. *Ibid.*, p. 37.

8. Vanessa Grigoriadis, "Rest the Tummy, Restore the Soul," *The New York Times* Magazine, August 24, 2003, p. 1.

9. *Ibid.*, p. 5.

10. *Ibid.*, p. 5.

11. G. W. Hunt, "Of Many Things" *America* Magazine, June 18-25, 1994.

12. Pierre Hegy and Joseph Martos, ed. *Catholic Divorce: The Deception of Annulments* (New York: Continuum, 2000) pp. 47, 48.

13. W. V. D'Antonio, J. D. Davidson, D. R. Hoge, and R. A. Wallace, *Laity American and Catholic: Transforming the Church* (Lanham, Michigan: Sheed and Ward, 1996), pp. 52-53.

14. "Protests Follow French bishop's Removal," National Catholic Reporter 31:20, January 27, 1995, p. 8.

15. Crossan, *ibid.*, p. 69.

16. E. P. Sanders, *Jesus And Judaism* (Philadelphia: Fortress Press, 1985), p. 206; see also Sanders, *The Historical Figure Of Jesus* (New York, New York: Penguin Books, 1995), pp. 232-237.

Chapter 4

From Being Helpless To Healing

Objective: To achieve a better understanding how we might carry on Jesus' healing ministry.

> *Then Jesus called the twelve together and gave them power and authority over all demons and to cure diseases, and he sent them out to proclaim the kingdom of God and to heal. He said to them, "Take nothing for your journey, no staff, nor bag, nor bread, nor money — not even an extra tunic. Whatever house you enter, stay there, and leave from there. Wherever they do not welcome you, as you are leaving that town shake the dust off your feet as a testimony against them." They departed and went through the villages, bringing the good news and curing diseases everywhere.*
>
> — Luke 9:1-6

When people go through significant transitions like a divorce, or a debilitating illness, or the death of a spouse, many feel helpless in addressing their own needs much less others' needs. They are truly in that never-never land we refer to as liminality. For example, after ten, twenty, or thirty years of bearing the persona of husband or wife, people who are recently divorced are legally no longer a husband or a wife. Yet, they need to go through the process of discovering who they are and valuing themselves apart from their previous relationship as a married couple. When they were married they had relied on one another to carry out certain tasks, e.g., financial matters, household chores, raising children. However, now that they are divorced, they often feel incompetent in making their own decisions. Some of the same problems occur if a person in a marriage dies. The difference between the breakup of a marriage, and the death of a spouse is that in an emergency the surviving spouse can't fall back on the deceased spouse.

While these examples illustrate how helpless some people feel when they experience loss intensely, they don't illustrate the helpless feelings another group of persons feel in the face of loss. These are the caregivers. They are going through their own liminal experiences of confusion and uncertainty as they care for a parent, son, daughter, or sibling suffering from a disease like Alzheimer's, AIDS, or some other debilitating illness. Day after day they watch helplessly as a loved one's health progressively deteriorates. The care-giver's loss is an anticipatory loss in which the caregiver grieves over the anticipated loss of the person who has given the caregiver meaning and purpose. Liminal experiences in which persons or their caregivers suffer loss are also occasions for depression. This isn't unusual. It is understandable that people become depressed when they experience loss. But depression intensifies the feeling of being helpless. However, does this mean being in this liminal or in-between phase of a transition inevitably means being helpless? Not necessarily.

While transitional experiences reveal how helpless we can become they can also help reveal in our helplessness a gift we all possess. What is that? A healing power comparable, although not identical, to Jesus' healing power. By reflecting on Jesus' commission to his disciples to heal, we shall discover in a transition the value of our liminal experiences to heal in a way we didn't think possible.

The journey passage from Luke's Gospel where Jesus commissions his disciples to heal is striking because he instructs them to take nothing with them on the journey. These instructions serve as an initiation into their healing ministry. Focusing on Jesus' instructions for the initial phase of their journey or transition gives us a piece of the puzzle how all Christians are enabled: "to proclaim the kingdom of God and to heal." In order to appreciate his instructions we need to view them within the context of Jesus' table ministry. We also need to see the difference between curing a disease and healing an illness.

Healing And Table Ministry

In chapter 2 we observed that Jesus did not exercise his healing ministry in one central location. Jesus "kept to the road" and "brought healing to those who needed it." Moreover, Jesus did not intend to hoard this ministry. Rather, his ideal was to heal people who would in turn become healers.

However, Jesus' healing ministry was also frequently connected to his table ministry. He healed others by gathering the whole and the unwhole alike to share table fellowship, and just as he expected those whom he healed to heal others, he also expected them to share table fellowship with whomever they healed:

> *Here is the heart of the original Jesus movement, a shared egalitarianism of spiritual (healing) and material (eating) resources. I emphasize this as strongly as possible, and I maintain that its materiality and spirituality, its facticity and symbolism, cannot be separated.* [1]

Whether we accept Crossan's conclusion or not, there is no reason to question Jesus' commission to his disciples to heal and be fed by those whom they healed as they traveled through the villages. But what kind of healing did Jesus expect his followers to do?

Curing A Disease And Healing An Illness

It is not my intention to become involved in a debate over whether Jesus actually healed people of physical diseases in all the instances recorded in the gospels. What is important here is the distinction medical anthropologists make between curing a disease and healing an illness. John Pilch states the difference succinctly:

> *Curing is the anticipated outcome relative to disease, that is, the attempt to take effective control of disordered biological and/or psychological processes. Healing is directed toward illness, that is the attempt to provide personal and social meaning for the life problems created by sickness.* [2]

The complaint that he has against modern biomedicine is that it is concerned only with the disease while the patient is searching for healing the illness. We might think because we bring a certain expertise through technology to cure someone's disease, we have addressed the needs of the whole person who has the disease. This simply isn't true. The difference between curing a disease and healing an illness is illustrated in the difference between determining how one can effect a cure for AIDS or the SARS epidemic, and how one can assist those who feel that they belong and are accepted in the community of the living. The problem in a technological age is that our successes in curing diseases might lead us to neglect what the disease means to the person who has it and how alienated from the community that person feels. To heal an illness is to address the anxieties, fears, and the isolation that the person experiences through the disease. A person might be healed of an illness without being cured of the disease, and vice versa.

It is this problem that personnel in Catholic hospitals need to address as they consider what it means to be identified as Catholic. Peter Steinfels cites two examples of major changes in the advance of technology over the last century that illustrate losses and gains in the health care system of Catholic hospitals when they change from a place of care to one of cure.

Two men had heart attacks, one in 1954 and the other in 1974. Both were taken to the same hospital. In 1954, the patient was placed under observation in a medical ward and released thirty-nine days later. He had a weakened heart that would burden him for years. In 1974, the second man went to the same hospital. Emergency resuscitation equipment was immediately available. Then the man was placed on an EKG monitor and put in intensive care. Fifteen days later he was released with an excellent prognosis:

The first patient declared that a "whole atmosphere of caring permeated the institution." The second patient reported that the care was impersonal and left him feeling lonely and isolated.[3]

In *Care of the Soul*, Thomas Moore makes a distinction between caring and curing which parallels the distinction between curing a disease and healing an illness. Care of the soul:

> *isn't about curing, fixing, changing, adjusting or making healthy, and it isn't about some idea of perfection or even improvement. It doesn't look to the future for an ideal, trouble-free existence.*[4]

> *A major difference between care and cure is that cure implies the end of trouble. If you are cured, you don't have to worry about whatever was bothering you any longer. But care has a sense of ongoing attention.*[5]

I am not suggesting that we must reinterpret all of Jesus' healing as healing solely the illness. We would certainly be missing the point of his healing activity if we restricted it to curing diseases. Our reflections on Jesus' reaching out to those who were marginalized revealed his healing as integrating the unhealed into the community. The evil that he opposed was not only physical but also social: the stigmatism which people experienced through being excluded from the community. He was passionate about integrating into the community those who were considered outsiders and felt alienated.

Combining Jesus' open table fellowship with this distinction between curing a disease and healing an illness sheds light on why Jesus instructed his disciples to take nothing for their journey — no staff, no bag, no bread, no money — not even an extra tunic. The most obvious reason was he desired his disciples to rely on divine providence for their provisions. They were to heal those who felt like outsiders and enjoy table fellowship provided by these people. Providence was to be experienced through the mutual dependence of guest and host in the exchange of healing and feeding.[6]

Further reflection on Jesus' healing activity and his instructions indicate how we might be healers in our communities through what must seem the antithesis of healing, namely, being helpless. But Jesus' words, "Take nothing for your journey, no staff, nor bag, nor bread, nor money — not even an extra tunic," suggests they had little to rely on when they did their healing. And as I have already suggested, those who feel like helpless caregivers are, in their own way, also healers. This brings us to the question: What are the healer's credentials?

The Healer's Credentials

Immersed in an age of specialization, our immediate reaction to Jesus' instructions provokes a host of questions. Why didn't he give his disciples a shopping list of what they needed to heal? If we had been there, wouldn't we have requested a few medical texts for easy reference or books of counseling with tips from Rogers, Jung, or Dr. Phil? Wouldn't we have drawn Jesus aside and politely pleaded for notes on listening skills, nodding wisely, and clarifying feelings? If we had been there wouldn't we have demanded tools of the trade? Stethoscopes, tongue depressors, band-aids, Tylenol, Mercurochrome! Wouldn't we have paraded our credentials? Our Ph.D.s, M.D.s, M.S.W.s? And the schools we attended? Harvard or Yale? But his instructions indicate that no degrees or special training is required in the art of healing. So if his disciples didn't bring anything with them — nothing in hand, or lodged in the folds of their tunics — how could they heal?

We might be tempted to console ourselves by recalling that these disciples were privileged to be around Jesus day in and day out, and since he had personally chosen them they must have been normal, sane, well-adjusted, dependable, mature people. Certainly they would not have been neurotic or dysfunctional! Jesus would not have made the mistake of sending out misfits to heal, would he? Unlike us they were whole and healthy, weren't they?

Or were they? Remember Peter? The loud mouth? Always promising more than he could deliver. Remember James and John? Talk about hotheads! They actually considered torching a whole town as a means of getting even with an inhospitable Samaritan village (Luke 9:54). Remember when these same brothers drew Jesus aside one day and asked if they could sit next to him, one on

68

his right and one on his left when they'd be together in the kingdom? (Mark 10:35-37). Talk about grandiose fantasies! But then, nearly all the disciples argued over who was the most important among them (Mark 9:34), and most of them weren't very brave. They all hightailed it when Jesus was arrested and went into hiding after his death. Wouldn't we recommend them for group therapy?

So we are left with our original question. Since his disciples didn't have the books, the credentials, or the rock-solid personalities, how did they heal? They seemed to have had nothing going for them. From our perspective they seemed pretty helpless! Here we need to pause and ask ourselves where we are coming from. It is we in the twenty-first century asking the question, and we are asking it as persons who assume technical expertise or at least psychological normalcy is required to be healers. So we leave healing to the professionals: the medical doctors and nurses, the psychologists, psychiatrists, social workers, ministers, or priests. But we do a disservice to ourselves and to those in need of healing if we assume that professional healers are automatically the best qualified to help others, and dismiss our own capacity to heal.

In *The Careless Society: Community and its Counterfeits*, John McKnight states we have abdicated our responsibility as healers by turning exclusively to the professionals. In the opening chapter he recounts the advent of the first bereavement counselor in a small Wisconsin town. Prior to the counselor's arrival the people:

> *mourned the death of a mother, brother, son, or friend. The bereaved were joined by neighbors and kin. They meet grief together in lamentation, prayer, and song. They called upon the words of the clergy and surrounded themselves with community.*[7]

But then the grief counselor arrived with the new grief technology. He assured the people of its superiority by presenting his credentials from a great university. As the counselor assumed more and more responsibility the townspeople assumed less and less:

> *The counselor's new tool will cut through the social fabric, throwing aside kinship, care, neighborly obligations,*

> *and community ways of coming together and going on
> ... the tools of bereavement counseling will create a
> desert where a community once flourished.*[8]

Robert Kegan offers a similar observation. Psychology has become the secular religion and practicing psychotherapy the new priestly rite. Then the impression is often conveyed that if we had a universal psychotherapy we would find a solution to all our ills:

> *The natural supports of family, peer groups, work roles,
> and love relationships come to be seen as merely ama-
> teur approximations of professional wisdom. From a
> developmental perspective this view of things is quite
> backward. Developmental theory has a long-standing
> appreciation of nature as the source of wisdom.*[9]

How are we to heal if we have nothing to fall back on? The indispensable tool for healing was, and still remains, the self: the compassionate self, in all its imperfection. That self, stripped of all pretense and game playing, is the most valuable asset of any healer. I am not thinking about the self that has gotten mended after a year or two of therapy. Nor am I thinking about persons who have their heads on straight and can give an eight-step program on being rehabilitated or recycled. Nor am I referring to those freed from anxiety, panic, and worry because they now have a surefire, unquestioned faith to guide them. The self which is the source of healing is not the heroic self that has kicked the habit and preaches to others that they can do it, too!

I am referring to the recovering alcoholic helping another through admitting to being a recovering alcoholic. Or the person navigating a stormy divorce accompanying other divorcing persons on their journeys. It is the healer's still-wounded self which alone speaks to the other's wound. The mother whose son has died of AIDS may well be the source of healing to another whose son or daughter has died of AIDS.

No one can be excused from being a healer. We cannot exempt ourselves because we are too young, too old, too ignorant, or too educated. Nor can we stand by because we don't think we have enough to say, or fear we'll say it poorly. There is no excuse because it is ultimately one's presence that heals, not smooth sounding words. People confined to hospital beds, nursing homes, or hospices are more in need of good listeners than of good speakers. Those who have recently lost a loved one are not making mental notes about the vocabulary or diction of those who visit and offer their sympathy.

Thus far we have seen how our preparation for becoming a healer involves a progressive stripping away of whatever we think we have needed to be a healer. But we would be deceiving ourselves if we thought we were finally prepared to be healers because we had arrived at the self and the self alone as the source of healing. The self is the source of healing but we are not referring to an isolated self, a self operating independently of others. This self is not an independent self but an interdependent self, especially in relation to the one being healed.

In all interaction between and among persons, as well as between and among everything in creation, there is interdependence. If we teach we can only do so because there are students who receive our teaching; if we preach it is only possible because there are those who receive our word and who in turn nourish us through their food which we call feedback. Interdependence means mutuality, reciprocity, and give and take. We discover our ability to heal in and through others who receive our healing. This discovery is an occasion for being thankful for what each of us can do for the other rather than what I can do for you or you for me. In other words, this discovery reveals that the transition from being helpless to healing means more than simply my healing the other. It means my being healed as well.

The idea that we are interdependent can be correlated with what we have learned about the disciples who were sent to heal people in their homes and who were in turn fed by them. Again we are reminded of Crossan's observation. "Here is the heart of the original Jesus movement, a shared egalitarianism of spiritual (healing) and material (eating) resources."

Jesus' recognition of interdependence is another way of stating that Jesus' healing always has a social dimension since the people whom he heals are integrated into the larger community. Being "healthy" is never a solitary matter. It is being-in-relation. Wendell Berry brings home the point that healing has a social dimension:

> *If we were lucky enough as children to be surrounded by grown-ups who loved us, then our sense of wholeness is not just the sense of completeness-in-ourselves, but is the sense also of belonging to others and to our place; it is an unconscious awareness of community, of having-in-common.*[10]

He says elsewhere:

> *I believe that the community — in the fullest sense: a place and all its creatures — is the smallest unit of health and that to speak of the health of an isolated individual is a contradiction in family or community or in a destroyed or poisoned ecosystem.*[11]

The Healer's Gifts

We have looked at what is essential to be a healer as well as the healer's mission of re-integrating others into the community. We have also seen that the healer must always prepare for healing by stripping him or herself of anything that might interfere with this process of healing. I would like to describe two concrete ways in which healing can take place: listening and touching.

Listening

Several years ago, at Georgetown University, an elderly lady set up a pup tent on the university campus. She placed a sign over the entrance of the tent that read, "I will listen to all of your problems for five cents." Students lined up outside the tent and as each student entered and then left other students asked, "What is she like?" "Tremendous! I felt so relieved! She really understood me! I want to go back to her!" What the students didn't realize was that the woman was deaf. Yes, she was deaf but she had a listening heart. She listened to the person. This story is instructive for two reasons. The first is that the woman who listens and heals through her listening is physically unable to hear. People who are physically impaired may or may not have a listening problem, just as people who can hear might not be able to listen. The second reason is that if the person in need of healing is to be integrated into the community, we must focus on the kind of healing which is essential. Being a member of the community means the person feels she or he belongs and is not an outsider. It is the person with heart, a listening heart who receives one who feels like an outsider into the community. Did Jesus and his disciples heal with listening hearts? Given Jesus' interest in the whole person and not simply in the person's physical well-being, we can presume that he intended to heal them of whatever prevented them from fully participating in the community.

Are we ever guilty of not listening with our hearts and of turning a deaf ear to someone in need of a listening heart? Someone going through a divorce or some other crisis? Certainly we turn a deaf ear when we refuse to give others a hearing. We tell them that we can't be bothered — we have more important things to do! Possibly we all do this from time to time. The danger is if we consistently turn a deaf ear we run the risk of never being reached, touched, or affected by others. Instead we dismiss others, minimize their needs, and become increasingly isolated. The process of not listening can begin slowly and innocently enough. But its results can be disastrous.

A case in point. Several years ago I decided I had a hearing problem and so I went to an ear, nose, and throat doctor. I told him I was worried because I frequently asked people to repeat themselves, "Huh? What was that you said?" or "I didn't hear you!" The doctor listened carefully to my story and then had the nurse administer a battery of tests to determine if I had suffered any hearing loss. Afterward I sat down, faced the doctor and anxiously waited his diagnosis. He smiled, scribbled something on a small piece of paper and handed it to me. I thought I was being given a prescription for my hearing problem. But no, there was only one sentence on the paper and it read, "Pay attention to people when they speak to you and you will have no hearing problem." Needless to say, I felt both relieved and ashamed. Relieved, because I had no physical impairment, but ashamed because I simply hadn't been listening to people who spoke to me. I had been given my warning about not listening. I sincerely hope I have changed. What this illustrates is the need to be vigilant lest we begin to turn a deaf ear on others without noticing it.

What does healing someone who is developing a deaf ear involve? It involves a conversion from turning a deaf ear to re-turning a listening heart. This conversion is accomplished when we are opened in such a way that an opening or clearing is prepared where others are free to enter our heart and have a favorable chance to be heard. How might this occur? The doctor who diagnosed my inattention scribbled a few words on a piece of paper. I believe these words created a small opening for me. Sometimes a breakdown in communication serves to remind us of our need to listen to how we aren't listening. When we get in heated discussions, we often think what we might say to win the argument rather than how open we might be to the other's point of view.

Like the elderly lady who listened to the college students, we too can listen to others by noticing non-verbal cues, e.g., facial expressions, bodily postures, and moods, in addition to what we hear with our ears. As this story illustrates there are times when we don't hear with our ears but we listen with our hearts.

All of us need a listening heart. Without a compassionate listener we might end up doing what I saw a bag lady do at five in the morning in a telephone booth on Madison Avenue in New York. She was talking loudly into the phone, reminding her non-existent partner at the other end of the line that she was John D. Rockefeller's daughter. It was a pathetic attempt on her part to be heard by someone even if that someone were a figment of her imagination. If we want to have heart-to-heart conversations with those in need then we need to have heart-to-heart listening.

Henri Nouwen contributes to our understanding the interdependent nature of healing through an article he had written on carrying for the elderly. In it, he gives the etymology of the word, care. It comes from the word *kara* which means to lament, to mourn, and to participate in suffering, to share in pain. Caring leads to community when the caregiver is conscious of his or her common brokenness with the one receiving care. For Nouwen, the professionals or those who cure, e.g., physicians, psychotherapists, and clergy, ought to understand that curing has to be undergirded by care. When it isn't, then the professionals and clients relate to each other as the:

> *powerful and the powerless, the knower to the ignorant, the have to the have not. The false silence of a doctor, the pretentious distance of a psychologist, and the self-righteous snobbery of a minister often inflict pains which hurt more than heal the wounds they want to cure.*[12]

Nouwen understands listening to be an interdependent activity in healing. Listening with care means the elderly person who tells his or her story discovers he or she has a story to tell and the one listening listens not only *to* a story but *with* a story. It is against the background of the listener's limited story that the listener discovers the uniqueness of the story he or she is privileged to hear. Then two lives come together in a healing way:

> *After a story is told and received with care, the lives of two people have become different. Two people have discovered their own unique stories and two people have become an integral part of a new fellowship.*[13]

It is also possible to observe listening as an interdependent healing activity among the elderly in a nursing home. Some of them gather and talk to one another about their life experiences prior to coming to the home. Often they repeat the same stories within a short span of time. Obviously they aren't aware they are retelling something about themselves, their children, or such. It doesn't seem to matter as each takes her turn listening and affirming whoever is telling her story. "Really? You don't say!" are simple statements but they are ways of affirming and being affirmed on the singular journey each has taken. Perhaps they are capable of ministering to one another in a way members of their own families cannot do precisely because these elderly persons don't recall having often spoken or heard the same stories.

When Jesus instructed his disciples on how to heal, they certainly had experienced in their own lives the healing power of Jesus' cry, *Ephphatha*, that is, "Be opened!" That is why they, too, could heal others' inability to listen. Being open is not something to be taken for granted. We, like they, can easily slip back into a pattern of not being open. It is necessary that even as we listen to the other, we listen to ourselves, as to whether or not we are listening with an open heart.

Touching

Jesus had the healing touch. Over and over we read how he healed through touch. Would he not have expected his disciples to do the same? The power of touch cannot be underestimated. However the healing touch is not just any kind of touch. Consider how we use the word touch to signify various kinds of intimacy and behavior. We want to "get in touch" with someone or we feel the need to "stay in touch." We are "touched" by a kind word or deed, and we are very "touchy" about certain topics. Someone who is vulnerable is a "soft touch" while a person who knows exactly what is needed in a particular situation has the "right touch." Some people add "a touch of class" to whatever they do.

However varied the usages, one thing is certain: Touching and being touched are necessary for our well-being. Babies and children need to be touched by their parents, particularly by their mothers, in a way that communicates warmth and affection. We have seen that the British psychiatrist, W. D. Winnicott speaks of the holding environment for the child, referring literally and metaphorically to the child's environment in which the mother holds or contains the child to communicate security. Children who are deprived of touch can suffer severe psychological problems.

But the need to touch and be touched doesn't stop when the child grows up, despite the fact that many people ignore that need once they reach adulthood. Interestingly, they develop what one observer has called skin hunger: A deep yearning for the touch that affirms, connects, assures, warms, and simply makes one feel "I belong." However, because of fears associated with touching and how that might be interpreted, touching is severely limited or disguised as when men slap one another on the back, or when athletes slap one another's posterior.

When there are no normal avenues of satisfying a pressing need, other ways will be found: "safe" ways. A voyeur "touches" another at a safe distance with his eyes, while others touch children. Even those whom we would consider normal might end up going to bed with veritable strangers, thinking they wanted sex when what they really wanted was simply the warm touch and reassuring presence of another person. In all these cases, it might well be an "empathic" touch that is desired. But what is the empathic touch?

Sally Gadow's insight on the healing touch caregivers might give their patients is helpful for all of us who heal and are healed in touching. The empathic touch is the touch of a person who enters into the world of another's meanings as a subject and not just as a subject touching an object. It is "the reality of the person" whom the caregiver touches, not the object of examination or manipulation. Nor is empathic touch the caregiver's attempt to bestow dignity. She considers this kind of touch to be philanthropic or asymmetrical. In the philanthropic paradigm:

> *Touch is a gift from one who is whole to one who is not. The indignity is not the affirmation of need in the other but its denial in oneself. In the empathic paradigm the subjectivity of the patient is assumed to be as whole and as valid as that of the caregiver.*[14]

We began this chapter by noting how striking it was that Jesus instructed his disciples to take nothing with them on the journey. They could rely on nothing but themselves and the saving power of Jesus' name although in the passage we quoted Jesus doesn't even mention himself as a source of their healing power. The source of healing was the self, the compassionate self of the disciple. The disciples Jesus sent listened through their wounds to the stories of the wounded persons they were sent to heal. Jesus was wise in sending these healers to the homes of others — wise in sending them without anything — because once they arrived and did their healing, they were hungry, and so they were dependent on their hosts at mealtime. There was reciprocity in these visits. Healing and eating were the exchanges and in the exchange the table fellowship took place. Both healer and healed were giving and receiving. Jesus knew exactly what he was doing when he sent his friends out with nothing at all. And what does this tell us about our ministry?

We are called to heal. No one can claim to be exempt because of some disability. We heal through our wounds, where we seem to be most helpless. When we listen to the other we tend and attend without trying to fix up and normalize. We heal, and in healing are healed in unexpected ways, through the very persons' presence to whom we are present. The relationship is one of interdependence.

As I have emphasized, we often discover our ability to heal in a liminal experience when we have been stripped of the means we usually employ in helping others or ourselves. These liminal experiences might precede our reaching out to help others, or we might discover them as we journey with others through their liminal experiences. In the latter instances it is only when we begin to feel that our noblest intentions to "help" the other are of no avail that we become healers. It is through our presence that we become a source of healing to others and they to us.

Exercises

1. Take about ten minutes to write how you felt when you not only helped someone but felt you had been helped in helping that person? Did you learn anything from this experience? Can you also recall a time when you helped someone in a manner which seemed insignificant to you, but later discovered how much it meant to the person you helped? Or a time when you thought you weren't helping a person at all, e.g., sitting helplessly with someone who was suffering, but later realizing how

important your presence was to that person? In all these instances of helping do you also see healing occurring? Do you think there is always a clear distinction between the healer and the healed?

2. Write down a time when you felt underappreciated by someone you helped or when you underappreciated another's help? If you felt underappreciated could you still rejoice in being able to experience what you had done for the other?

Questions For Discussion

1. Have you ever thought of yourself as having healing abilities? Here we understand healing abilities not as the power of one person to heal another but the experience of healing and being healed by the one who reaches out to help another. This is the interdependence of healing — of both healer and healed mutually benefiting from the activity. To touch another (psychologically, spiritually, physically) in a way that you are healed by the other's receptive response is an interdependent activity. On the other hand, touching another from a power position is not healing in an interdependent sense. While it is true that the physician exercises his power with his probing instruments, healing the person as person means the physician doesn't simply regard the person as an object to be manipulated. If touch means, "Look what I am doing for you!" regardless of what it means to the one being touched there is no interdependence of touch here. If touch is intrusive or manipulative, it may be nothing more than the exercise of one's power and therefore abusive.

2. Listening is another instance of interdependence. Can you recall a time when listening to another's story or concern you not only lent an ear to the other but you also felt privileged to enter that person's world in a way no one else had done? When someone is grieving and asks if he or she can speak to you

about his or her loss, wouldn't you say that healing takes place in both of you even if the healing is hardly noticeable at the time?

3. Have you ever healed through your wounds? Through your feelings of loss have you been able to reach out to someone experiencing a similar loss? Have you ever been addicted to alcohol or drugs and joined a group like Alcoholics Anonymous? Weren't you healing and being healed through your wounds? Are you a widow or a widower or have you gone through a divorce and discovered that in sharing your story as well as listening to others' mutual healing took place? On the other hand, if you are no longer in touch with your wounds and have "overcome" your problem are you any longer healing through your wounds as you proudly tell others how you have overcome your problem?

---

1. Dominic Crossan, *Jesus: A Revolutionary Biography* (San Francisco: Harper-Collins, 1994), p. 107.

2. John Pilch, *Healing In The New Testament: Insights from Medical and Mediterranean Anthropology* (Minneapolis: Fortress Press, 2000) p. 25.

3. Peter Steinfels, *A People Adrift: The Crisis of the Roman Catholic Church in America* (New York: Simon & Schuster, 2003), p. 117.

4. Thomas Moore, *Care Of The Soul* (San Francisco: HarperCollins, 1992), p. xv.

5. *Ibid.*, pp. 18, 19.

6. Crossan, *ibid.*, pp. 118, 119.

7. John McKnight, *The Careless Society: Community And Its Counterfeits* (New York: Basic Books, 1995), p. 5.

8. *Ibid.*, pp. 6, 7.

9. Robert Kegan, *The Evolving Self* (Cambridge: Harvard University Press, 1982), p. 255.

10. Wendell Berry, "Health Is Membership" *Utne Reader*, Sept.-Oct., 1995, p. 95.

11. *Ibid.*, p. 61.

12. Sally Gadow, "Touch And Technology: Two Paradigms of Patient Care," *Journal Of Religion And Health*, Vol. 23, Spring, 1984, p. 68.

13. Henri Nouwen, "Care And The Elderly," *Aging And The Human Spirit* (Chicago, Illinois: Exploration Press), p. 293.

14. *Ibid.*, p. 294.

Chapter 5

From A Center Destroyed To A Center Renewed

Objective: To understand how we might gain a deeper appreciation of the function of the shadow in our lives by considering how it manifests in our daily lives.

*Just then a lawyer stood up to test Jesus. "Teacher," he
said, "what must I do to inherit eternal life?" He said
to him, "What is written in the law? What do you read
there?" He answered, "You shall love the Lord your
God with all your heart, and with all your soul, and
with all your strength, and with all your mind; and your
neighbor as yourself." And he said to him, "You have
given the right answer, do this, and you will live." But
wanting to justify himself, he asked Jesus, "And who is
my neighbor?" Jesus replied, "A man was going down
from Jerusalem to Jericho, and fell into the hands of
robbers, who stripped him, beat him, and went away,
leaving him half dead. Now by chance a priest was going
down that road; and when he saw him, he passed by on
the other side. So likewise a Levite, when he came to
the place and saw him, passed by on other side. But a
Samaritan while traveling came near him; and when
he saw him, he was moved with pity. He went to him
and bandaged his wounds, having poured oil and wine
on them. Then he put him on his own animal, brought
him to an inn, and took care of him. The next day he
took out two denarii, gave them to the innkeeper, and
said, 'Take care of him; and when I come back, I will
repay you whatever more you spend.' Which of these
three, do you think, was a neighbor to the man who fell
into the hands of the robber?" He said, "The one who
showed him mercy." Jesus said to him, "Go and do
likewise."*   — Luke 10:25-37

In our transitions we often overlook our inner conflicts because we are focused on the more obvious ones with persons in our outer world. But within ourselves an almost imperceptible evolution of different voices, i.e., ideas and attitudes that contradict what has give meaning to our lives, can easily be confused with others' ideas that threaten what we value. For example, we might idealize and defend a religious figure whom others criticize without our being aware of a growing conflict within ourselves about this person's integrity. Periodically, we find ourselves questioning the wisdom of the person we've admired, but quickly dismiss these thoughts, or alien voices, as testing our loyalty to this person. However, gradually, our conflicted feelings become more intense between inner familiar voices that have commanded allegiance, and inner alien voices that now demand a hearing. When this happens we are deep into the in-between stage of a transition because increasingly our world of meaning is not secure.

During transitions we help ourselves by becoming sensitive not only to others' needs with whom we dialogue in the outer world, but also with the invisible others dwelling within. By dialoguing with these inner voices that challenge us to reexamine what has centered us or given meaning we could either deepen our appreciation of what had given meaning or discover a new center of meaning.

One of the journey stories, which is most helpful in illustrating the voices in both our inner and outer world, is the story of the Good Samaritan. For Christians, this is one of the most familiar stories in the Bible either because we have been helped by a good Samaritan or been one ourselves.

However, familiarity with the story might also prevent us from gaining a fresh perspective on it. For example, what generally appeals is the idea that the Samaritan is a good person, but what we fail to appreciate is the longstanding enmity between Jew and Samaritan. For that reason we might be unaware of how problematic it was for Jews to receive help from any Samaritan no matter how good the Samaritan might have been. Failing to recognize this, we miss the real challenge the story presents.

By focusing on the journey as a transitional story in which the wounded man confronts his enemy, we can explore the role of conflict as a potential for self-renewal. By "self," I mean our center or inner holy of holies that gives meaning to our lives. Like our other journey stories, this one follows the pattern of separation, liminality, and reincorporation. The traveler leaves Jerusalem (separation), is robbed somewhere between Jerusalem and Jericho (in-betweenness), and concludes his journey at an inn (reincorporation).

As we proceed through each phase of the journey we'll be observing background, events, and characters first on one level and then on another. The two levels are the interpersonal and the intrapersonal. As already noted, usually we only think of relating interpersonally through our interaction with others in the outer world. We don't think of interacting intrapersonally, but each of us has an inner world with its cast of characters — what Carl Jung called the little people of the psyche, or Mary Watkins described as "invisible guests," or Elizabeth O'Connor's, "our many selves." While occasionally we notice how we relate intrapersonally we do so less frequently than we do interpersonally. Even as we are relating interpersonally, we are carrying on internal dialogues with ourselves. (A reflection on the rationale for noticing the presence of, and dialoguing with these inner others appears at the end of this chapter.)

Here we begin our reflection on the story of the Good Samaritan by briefly reading it as an intrapersonal dialogue or as relating to the different voices within one's self.

"I was on my way down from Jerusalem to Jericho when I fell into my own hands. I stripped myself, beat myself, and went away, leaving myself half dead. Now by chance I was going down the road. When I saw myself, I passed by on the other side. Again, I came to the place where I lay and again I passed by on the other side. Finally I came near to myself, and when I saw myself I was moved with pity. I bandaged my wounds and poured oil and wine on them. Then I carried myself to an inn where I took care of myself. The next day I gave myself two denarii to take care of myself, and I promised to pay myself more later if this were needed."

Admittedly this revision sounds awkward, but as a commentary on the intrapersonal level the story yields interesting insights.

However, before looking at this story on both intrapersonal and interpersonal levels, some background information is necessary.

The distance between Jerusalem and Jericho is about seventeen miles, and the route runs through desert and rocky hill country. It is wild and barren, and the road between the two cities was a notorious hideout for bandits. It is no wonder that anyone traveling on that road would have been robbed.

The characters in the story are the man who was robbed, the robbers, the priest, the Levite, the Samaritan, and an innkeeper. We know nothing about the traveler's personal life since he was stripped of all means of identification. He had no clothes that would have indicated his socio-economic status or ethnic background. We can assume he was Jewish, like the audience Jesus addressed.

The priest and the Levite might have been returning to Jericho from their Temple duties since Jericho was a city where many of the priests lived when they weren't performing their duties in Jerusalem. One reason often given for their not coming to the assistance of the injured man is that they would have been made ritually unclean if they touched what appeared to be a corpse. Their whole life was devoted to being pure since they had to be ritually clean to perform their Temple duties. However according to the Mishnah and Talmud burying a neglected corpse would not have defiled them. Whatever their motivation, the audience hearing Jesus (largely Jewish peasants) would not have sympathized with these urban elite clerics. The priest's and the Levite's motivation is of no major concern here. What is important is their presence in the story as representatives of the purity system.

The Samaritan in any case would never have been considered pure. Samaritans had traditionally been mortal enemies of the Jews. After the Babylonian exile the Samaritans had opposed the restoration of Jerusalem and in the second-century B.C. had helped the Syrian rulers in their wars against the Jews. In Sirach (50:25-26), written about 200 B.C., the Samaritans are called "no nation," and in 128 B.C. the Jewish high priest burned the Samaritan temple on Mount Gerizim. In the early first-century A.D. the Samaritans scattered the bones of a corpse in the temple during Passover, defiling the temple and preventing the celebration of the feast.[1]

The Jews considered themselves socially, racially, and religiously superior to the Samaritans. While Jews and Samaritans both claimed Abraham as their ancestor, the Jews regarded the Samaritans as unholy. "He that eats the bread of the Samaritans is like to one who eats the flesh of swine," expressed their sentiment (Mishnah).

What would have made the Samaritan in this story even more repugnant was his occupation. A Samaritan traveling back and forth in Judean territory may have been a trader, a despised occupation. Indication of his being a trader is the fact that he possesses oil, wine, and considerable funds. Many traders were wealthy, having grown rich at the expense of others. They were, therefore, considered thieves and frequented the inns.[2]

The innkeeper was given the responsibility of looking after the wounded man while the Samaritan was away. The inns "were notoriously dirty and dangerous and run by persons whose public status was below even that of traders. Only people without family or social connections would ever risk staying at a public inn."[3]

Separation From The Center

Interpersonal

The traveler was on his way down to Jericho from Jerusalem, the religious and political center of the country. Jerusalem was the holy city, the center of the universe for the Jew. To be in relation to the center was to be in relation to what gave meaning and direction. Traveling away from the center into the wilderness meant traveling into what was chaotic and unholy.

However, as we observed in discussing the purity system in chapter 3, the religious elite in Jerusalem decided what it meant to be holy. We have seen how equating holiness with wholeness favored the elitist. Holiness was to be mediated through observance of laws associated with the purity system. Well intentioned as the pious Jew's motivation might have been to approximate the holiness of God, undue emphasis on this value and the means of achieving it meant few were holy and many unholy. The danger of extolling holiness to the exclusion of other values like compassion and mercy could easily become a form of idolatry.

Intrapersonal

Often, people are tempted to idolize someone or some thing as the center or inner sanctum of their lives. Their primary concerns, fantasies, and ambitions are connected with this center. When there is a possibility of, or threat to losing this center, in reality it is a representation of the holy that is being threatened. The representation has a numinous, compelling quality about it that gives meaning and centers the person. This could be a belief system, an authoritative interpretation of who, or what, God is. What held meaning need not explicitly have had anything to do with God. An ideology, career, relationship, or special project might become a sacred center that holds meaning. However, a serious crisis related to this center could lead to a descent into the wilderness that we might liken to the traveler's dangerous journey between Jerusalem and Jericho.

Devoid Of A Center

Interpersonal

It is in the wilderness where the traveler is robbed, stripped, beaten, and left half dead. We read that first a priest and then a Levite sees him, but neither of them stops to help him. The kindest interpretation is that these men were torn between assisting someone who appeared to be dead, and following what they thought the law required of them. The worst interpretation is that they simply didn't care to become involved. They might also have been fearful that robbers were close by waiting to attack anyone who stopped to assist the traveler. Whatever their reasons, they continued on their journey.

The turning point in the story is the arrival of the Samaritan. We might think someone as badly beaten as the traveler would have welcomed the Samaritan's presence. But that is our perspective, not a Jew's. The biblical scholar John Pilch observed that a pious Jew believed it was against God's will to receive a kindness from non-Jewish enemies. So, technically, following the purity laws it would have been a curse, not a blessing to receive assistance from the Samaritan. He was impure religiously, racially, and socially. Moreover, the oil and wine that the Samaritan poured into the Jew's wounds would have been repugnant to him since they were not kosher.

Situations approximating this aren't too difficult to imagine: a Palestinian receiving assistance from an Israeli; a Tutsi being comforted by a Hutu in Rwanda; an American soldier being aided by a Taliban.

Intrapersonal

How does the traveler's plight mirror our journey? When we lose whatever has been our center of meaning it is as if we have been stripped of our identity. If we lose someone through death, or divorce, or if we retire we might suffer narcissistic injuries to ourselves. Since we see and value ourselves in varying degrees through others' eyes, when the other leaves the scene our self-esteem plummets. We might react negatively by considering ourselves unlovable, and belittling our achievements as amounting to nothing. Then we end up falling prey to our own abuse. Here the expression, "We become our own worst enemy" takes on special meaning.

Even having sustained these injuries we often do nothing to tend our wound. Like the priest and the Levite we notice but prefer not to get close to our wound. We don't seek help. Surprisingly, many people suffer depression for years rather than seeking help because this would be an admission of weakness.

Given the description of the Samaritan on the interpersonal level as unholy, because he represents what is religiously, socially, and racially different, on the intrapersonal level we can identify the Samaritan as the wounded man's *shadow*. In Jungian psychology the shadow is the unacknowledged side of the personality. It is the opposite of how we see ourselves. If we present ourselves as committed believers, there is a side of us that doesn't buy all this religion! Or if we think of ourselves as the pacifist there is a side that is combative. But the converse might also be true. The combative person might not be consciously aware of his or her pacifistic tendencies. In other words what goes unacknowledged and undeveloped becomes part of the shadow. This is because certain qualities or feelings are not considered acceptable by the individual within the context of family or society that regards these qualities as unacceptable.

The shadow develops secretly alongside certain conscious attitudes, ideas, perspectives that we identify as being mine, me, the way I think. Conflicting ideas, beliefs, and perspectives are repressed because they are simply considered unacceptable in my family, my religion, or my society. Families that are more introverted might regard a highly extroverted son or daughter as too demonstrative or ebullient and therefore encourage or demand their child exercise self-restraint. Consequently the child learns it is in his or her best interest not to be so extroverted. But these extroverted energies don't just disappear. They become part of that person's shadow. We might be well intentioned in encouraging children to be kind and loving, but if there isn't any outlet for their "negative" feelings these can end up being part of their shadow. Opinions and ideas that are unacceptable within the context of family and society don't simply go away. They go underground. So we identify with what we consciously hold to be true, and what goes contrary to our belief becomes shadow. But just because these feelings aren't conscious doesn't mean that they have no power. They are alive in the unconscious.

It is when we are unaware of our shadow that it is potentially destructive. Without being aware, we begin to see in others what we fail to see in ourselves. We project our shadow onto others. For example if we are sexually attracted to someone but unable to admit this attraction, we might imagine others having strong sexual feelings toward this person by interpreting others' innocent remarks as sexually motivated. Then we might warn this person of others' devious intentions. Another indication we are projecting our shadow are the intense negative feelings compelling us to berate the other. It is as if the one on whom we had projected our shadow were some terrible itch that we obsessively kept scratching.

We project our sins onto minorities, other nationalities, and other religions. All that is noble and good is on our side and all that is ignoble and bad is on the other side. *They* are lazy and lecherous; we are not. We tell the truth; they tell lies. We are children of the light and they are children of the dark. This is scapegoating. Scapegoating is deadly when it involves one race, nation, or religion against another.

Parenthetically, it is important to add that we not only project negative attributes onto others but we also project positive attributes. We might admire someone as being very courageous or charming and not realize we ourselves are courageous or charming in many ways. We might see in a spouse all the strengths we think we lack. Often it is only when someone's spouse dies that the person begins to see that he or she actually has the ability to do what the deceased spouse could do.

So the shadow is very powerful when it remains unconscious and is projected onto others. We need to become aware of our projections. Then we are in a position to recognize that *we* harbor undreamed of attitudes, feelings, and abilities we had projected onto others.

How can our understanding of the shadow be helpful in understanding the Samaritan from an intrapersonal perspective? We began reflecting on the loss of a center as the loss of what we had regarded as most "holy" in our lives. The Samaritan represents what is racially, religiously, and socially different from the Jew. While these differences were offensive to the Jew they were also potentially liberating insofar as they offered different perspectives on life. For the Jew to be whole and therefore holy meant excluding what was different. However, there is another way of looking at wholeness or perfection. Wholeness or integrity can also be defined as *embracing* differences and polarities. When Jesus tells his disciples, "You must therefore be perfect just as your heavenly Father is perfect" (Matthew 5:48), the word perfect is open to misunderstanding. John Sanford explains that the Greek word in question (*teleios*) does not mean "purity" but completeness. What Jesus is urging is that our lives and our personalities be brought to completeness. This completeness means recognizing our shadow personality. However the recognition of the shadow involves an

> *acceptance of this personality as a troublesome, but basically helpful part of our totality. The solution to the shadow problem that Jesus offers us, then, involves the growth of psychological consciousness and spiritual maturity by the recognition of our darkness, as well as our light.*[4]

Commenting on the same biblical passage David Steindl-Rast writes that:

> *Jesus stresses the fact that God obviously allows the interplay of shadow and light. God approves of it. If God's perfection allows for tensions to work themselves out, who are we to insist on a perfection in which all tensions are suppressed?*[5]

By becoming aware of how we project our shadow onto others we can begin to see ourselves in a different light. Consciously we are identified so strongly with one perspective that we are blinded to others, which might moderate or even complement our own perspective that has become too narrow or rigid. Over a period of years unchallenged assumptions and attitudes can become very oppressive since we are reduced to seeing ourselves and our world through limited frames of reference. This can manifest itself personally in our refusal to be conciliatory towards family and friends whose lifestyle is at variance with ours. We think that if we open our hearts or minds to those who see things differently we shall become contaminated and unprincipled. "You want to go and shack up with somebody? That's your business but don't expect your mother and me to keep the home fires burning for you!" Or, "As far back as I can remember no one on my side of the family has gotten a divorce, and if you get one don't bother to come here for sympathy!" Admitting no compromise, we become purists in politics or religion. "I don't care! It's immoral to use condoms! There's no two ways about it. People won't get AIDS if they just use some restraint!" Or, "They're giving in! They're compromising! I tell you friends, if you give an inch here you'll lose everything!" Liberal and conservative politicians have a field day seeing the enemy in each other.

Our awareness of the Samaritan, the other within, dawns when the shadowy stuff begins to make its appearance in our doubting, questioning, negative reactions, and sense of disillusionment toward what we had considered the truth. "You know ... I hadn't realized it but I've had to face the fact that there's more than one way of looking at it. I hate to say it but I think I envy them. I guess I've always wanted to be as free as they are and didn't have the courage to do what they've done!" The Samaritan embodies our own "inner other." What we had seen only as an outer threat in those people out there we are now beginning to see as "our" other speaking to us from within.

In the story, the alien whom the wounded man's culture regarded as flawed helped him. The Samaritan who showed compassion through the ministrations of oil and wine initiated the process of healing. It contrasts remarkably with the process of making whole through ritual purification and the avoidance of anything or anyone impure. Considered a source of contamination himself, the Samaritan healed the man through his action. Moreover, the oil and wine that he used weren't only standard first-aid remedies. They were also sacrificial elements in the Temple worship. The Jewish priest and Levite were the religious professionals who knew the precise rituals of the prescribed liturgy. In worship they officiated at the sacrifices and libations. They poured out the oil and the wine on the high altar before God. Bailey observes:

> *Here in the parable this same freighted language is applied to the Samaritan just after the priest and Levite have failed miserably in their ability to make the "living sacrifice." It is the hated Samaritan who pours out the libation on the altar of this man's wounds.*[6]

This story illustrates that healing or becoming whole is not achieved through avoiding others who are unwhole. Rather healing takes place through embracing what is different. Becoming whole is not a progressive narrowing in which the more whole or holy we are the fewer the people there are like ourselves with whom we can associate.

Commenting on the difference between genuine community and its counterfeit (lifestyle), the authors of *Habits Of The Heart* write:

> *Whereas a community attempts to be an inclusive whole, celebrating the interdependence of public and private life and of the different callings of all, lifestyle is fundamentally segmental and celebrates the narcissism of similarity. It usually explicitly involves a contrast with others who "do not share one's lifestyle."*[7]

Making whole is a progressive expansion or inclusion of what is different, other, and alien through the agency of compassion. Implicit is the idea that "my" wholeness or integrity is meaningless unless it expands to a vision of "our" wholeness. To be "catholic" is not to be narrowly sectarian and exclusive but universal, inclusive. While the story illustrates this on the interpersonal level it is also instructive on the intrapersonal level.

We need to be in touch with the "unholy" in ourselves — the strange, the alien — if we are to be genuinely holy. To become psychologically conscious and face our shadow to the extent this is possible is not easy or enjoyable. But it is a task whose goal is integrating our inner other as well as purifying the air of our relationship with others so that we might embrace others in their otherness. Jesus tells us that we are called to love our neighbor as our self. We see why this is no small task as we become aware of dimensions of the self we had no idea existed.

Reincorporation Of A Renewed Center

Interpersonal
But there is more to the story. The Samaritan takes the wounded man to an inn. Earlier we observed that inns were dirty, dangerous, and run by persons whose public status was below even that of

traders. Only people without family or social connections would risk staying at a public inn. Hence, we can assume the man's recovery continues in an atmosphere that is unholy since the inn and its inhabitants are hardly respectable. How are we to understand this conclusion? To appreciate what is happening at the inn we recall what had happened to this man. He had left Jerusalem, the center of a holiness mediated through the purity system by the religious elite. However valuable a vehicle it might have been for genuinely worshiping God, it could also become an obstacle creating problems for people unable to meet the criteria for being whole.

He traveled down a road into the wilderness. There he was wounded, stripped of his identity, and left to die. Aid came from an unholy source, the Samaritan, and he was brought to an unholy place for recovery. But what did he recover? Presumably he recovered his health, his wholeness. Being indebted to the Samaritan might have led him to understand being whole (and therefore holy) didn't mean avoiding contact with what was other, different, strange, or unholy. On the contrary, he could have gained the insight that what he had believed to be contaminating had actually helped him become whole.

However, his recovery would have been a mixed blessing. His experience of being helped by his enemy might also have left him confused, maybe even frightened. Negative reactions to his new relationship with this Samaritan might even have led him to believe it would have been better if he had died. Of course he might also have begun to realize that in spite of confusing reactions, his experience was helping him to see a connection to the "enemy" which others around him might never see.

From the perspective of what had traditionally been considered holy, the inn was unholy. But from another perspective it was possible to view the inn in a positive way. At the inn, the wounded man's continued exposure to those who were different from him was an ongoing challenge to relate to them. Considerably different from the center in Jerusalem cleansed of "impurity," this center was both available to and operated by people who were considered impure. The relationship between him and the others could be one of continuing hostility or fruitful exchange. If the latter occurred, the inn would become a new center of meaning distinguished from the old by the integration of differences into a new, complex unity.

Intrapersonal

The possibilities of interpretation on the interpersonal level are mirrored in the possibilities offered on the intrapersonal. Those possibilities I have described in giving a rationale for entering into dialogue with the inner others who populate our inner life. It is they who frequent the inn. They are the ones we treat as impure when we refuse to acknowledge their presence. By our refusal we make enemies of them as surely as we make enemies of people whom we treat with indifference in our outer world.

Ongoing intrapersonal dialogue facilitates the connection with one's Self as Carl Jung understood the Self. The Self is not to be identified with the side of ourselves, which we ordinarily refer to as "myself," or the "me" I know best. Since the Self is difficult to define because it refers to both the conscious and unconscious and their collaboration, it is more helpful to describe it in images. One especially helpful image of the inn is that of the kingdom of God. In response to a question of the Pharisees about when the kingdom of God would come, Jesus answered, "The kingdom of God is not coming with things that can be observed, nor will they say, 'Look, here it is!' or 'There it is!' For, in fact, the Kingdom of God is among you" (Luke 17:20-21). For Elizabeth Boyden Howes, the translation "within you" refers to the kingdom as both inner and outer reality. What is possible about the reign of God in human society also has its counterpart in the individual psyche. "Thus, all the qualities that characterize the kingdom as social or outer community also describe an inner reality. The social reality of the kingdom also has a parallel in the psyche."[8]

Whether we take the image of the inn and the kingdom of God as ways of relating interpersonally or intrapersonally, these images both refer to an expansion of our awareness beyond "our kind." Neither our interpersonal nor intrapersonal relationships by themselves are capable of expanding this awareness. We cannot become aware of our inner world of dark, ominous strangers except first through our projections of these inner others onto outer others whom

96

we often unfairly conclude are enemies. But neither can we see others as they are except by recognizing that what we have judged to be ominous in them comes from our inner world of strangers.

The purity issues which need our attention have nothing to do with avoiding inner or outer others whose presence threaten us. Rather we ought to be concerned about polluting the moral atmosphere through shadow projections and counter projections. By "owning" the inner others, which we have disclaimed in our projections, we experience ever more deeply our own center. We are reconnected simultaneously on inner and outer levels with the kingdom of God, our new holy of holies. We can conclude this reflection on the Good Samaritan by quoting Donohue's appraisal of the story:

> It challenges us to move beyond our social and religious constructs of good and evil; it subverts our tendency to divide the world into insiders and outsiders. It makes us realize that goodness may be found precisely in those we most often call evil or enemy.[9]

Reflection: The Intrapersonal Dialogue

In order to dialogue with the different voices of the self we need to become reacquainted with the different ways in which they speak to us. This is another way of saying that we need to listen in a new way to the inner voices that want to be heard. For example, driving on the highway we might hear the speed demon within muttering, "Get out of my way," as we pass others by, or we might hear in our own voice the victim complaining about all who are determined to take advantage of us as they "intentionally" weave in front of us. Or, the therapist in us might appear as we offer friendly counsel to a friend in need. Not only do we experience the presence of these others in our words, when they appear we might even detect changes in our body: in our gait as the hero swaggers to do battle with the boss, or in our posture as the victim slouches and whimpers over life's trials.

Some of these inner others appear in our dreams as different characters who are friendly, jealous, desperate, or cowardly. Certain situations invariably bring the same voice on stage center. At age fifty we might almost always hear the child revive when we're visiting a mother or father who gives us familiar warnings about what we should or shouldn't eat. All these others are potential partners for the dialogue. Some are more insistent on being heard than others and often one will drown out all the others for days on end. While our hero always seems intent on saving others, our victim seems determined to be forever victimized.

We might think that all this talk about inner voices is okay for children who have imaginary playmates. We might even concede that a segment of the population, the schizophrenics, can carry on conversations with people who aren't there because of their condition. We think it childish to dialogue as children do with imaginary playmates, and simply mad to mimic habits of the sick. However, by dismissing dialogue out of hand we dismiss our artists and our saints. For novelists, playwrights, and people of prayer do not find it childish to carry on dialogues with invisible partners. They know how well their lives have been enriched by listening and entering into dialogue with their voices. Are they immature?

The real danger lies not in taking these voices seriously but in ignoring them. In doing so we unwittingly insult them and provoke them into endlessly disrupting our lives. Our refusal to acknowledge their presence may lead to the result that one or the other begins to tyrannize our consciousness. When the victim needs a hearing and we ignore its voice we may be plagued daily by it. Finally we end up identifying with the victim. The danger, then, is not in being fragmented by these voices but in refusing to dialogue and be enriched by their presence.

Imagine sitting around a table talking and listening to one another. Someone who is ignored or feels frozen out of the conversation changes slowly from quiet to sullen, to angry to disruptive. But giving them a fair hearing can completely alter this dynamic. Others won't be so contentious if they know they will be heard. Listening to them we realize that each has something important to say which we might otherwise have overlooked. Might there not be a time to be the victim and a time to be the hero? A time to be passive and a time to act? As long as none of the voices claim the right to be the only voice, we are free to enjoy multiple perspectives on others and ourselves. But if the voices at the table are forbidden ever to speak up or if one or two insist, "I alone exist," then inevitably there will be increasing tension and isolation as they all turn their backs on one another. This inner alienation is known as a multiple personality disorder. The disorder does not center on the fact that there are multiple voices within us, but that they are not in dialogue with one another.

In transitions we hear voices that we have not heard before. They might be strong; they might be weak. Some might be strident because they have seldom been given a hearing. But once heard, these same voices might become conciliatory. Like so many of our friends or neighbors these inner others are not always what they seem. They can change if given a chance to be heard. In this respect they are not unlike the people outside of ourselves with whom we also dialogue and grow in understanding.

Exercises

1. Write down the name of a person whom you extremely dislike. That person can be someone you know personally or it might be someone who is in politics, the movies, or on television. For a couple of minutes describe what it is you dislike so intensely about this person. Describe your feelings. Be as concrete as possible. Do this before you continue writing.

   After you have written what you dislike in this person so strongly ask yourself if there is anything, which you dislike in this person that might be present in your own personality. If there is, it might reveal itself in unguarded moments, or through a friend telling you something about yourself that resembles what you see in the person you dislike. Write down what it is you dislike in the other that might be present in yourself. This might indicate something of your shadow.

2. Now take the time to spend a few minutes describing someone whom you admire intensely whether or not you personally know this person. It could be a friend or it could be someone in politics, the movies, or on television. After you have done this ask yourself if there is anything you admire in this person that potentially is present within yourself which has gone unacknowledged. You have discovered something of your "golden" shadow within yourself that needs to be developed.

Questions For Discussion

1. Do religious wars often result from negative projections, i.e., seeing all that is evil in another religion and only all that is good within one's own religion? Do we tend to see everything in terms of black or white, good or bad, right or wrong with the negative projections taking place in persons, institutions, or other things we don't like?

2. In the story of the Good Samaritan we saw that owning one's shadow can enrich one's personality, not destroy it. There is hidden potential for growth in the shadow. Thus, someone who is overly dependent is neglecting to develop a side that could be assertive or someone who is overly independent might be harboring a need to rely more on others than that person is consciously willing to acknowledge. Can you think of something within yourself that you might possibly develop but don't because you don't think of yourself as having that need? Isn't it true that we might live in a culture in which men are unwilling to express their feelings openly because it is deemed unmanly? Then the cultural shadow would be the repression of these feelings?

---

1. John R. Donahue, SJ, *The Gospel In Parable* (Minneapolis: Fortress Press, 1988), p. 130.

2. Bruce J. Malina and Richard Rohrbaugh, *Social-Science Commentary On The Synoptic Gospels* (Minnepolis: Fortress Press, 1992), p. 346.

3. Malina, *ibid.*, p. 347.

4. John Sanford, "Jesus, Paul And Depth Psychology," *Religious Education* Vol. XLVIII, No. 6, November-December, 1973, p. 11.

5. David Steindl-Rast, "The Shadow In Christianity," *Meeting The Shadow* (Los Angeles, California: Tarcher, 1991), p. 132.

6. Kenneth E. Bailey, *Through Peasant Eyes* (Grand Rapids: Eerdmans, 1980), p. 50.

7. Robert Bellah, et al, *Habits Of The Heart* (Berkeley: University of California Press, 1985), p. 72.

8. Elizabeth Boyden Howes, *Jesus' Answer To God* (San Francisco: Guild For Psychological Studies Publishing House, 1984), pp. 95, 96.

9. Donahue, *ibid.*, p. 134.

Chapter 6

From God Manageable To Godawful

Objective: To become more aware of how we often demand that God live up to our image of who God ought to be for us rather than letting God be God in God's own way.

> *But the Lord sent a large fish, that swallowed Jonah and he remained in the belly of the fish three days and three nights.* — Jonah 2:1

Many major crises generated in transitions involve us in a conflict with God. These conflicts often undermine our assumptions about who this God is we worship. While some of our experiences are profoundly satisfying, others are so disturbing that we would not identify them as coming from God. The reason is we have learned from our parents, our teachers, and our churches that God is a gentle, caring father who is our friend and protector.

Important as these images are in helping us appreciate the God we worship, they don't show us the "dark" side of God. We seem to be blissfully unaware of Jacob's struggle with God at the Jabbok (Genesis 32:22-32). Nor do we ponder Job's complaint over God's heavy-handed dealings with him.

> *Therefore I will not restrain my mouth; I will speak in the anguish of my spirit; I will complain in the bitterness of my soul. Am I the Sea, or the Dragon, that you set a guard over me? When I say, "My bed will comfort me, my couch will ease my complaint," then you scare me with dreams and terrify me with visions, so that I would choose strangling and death rather than this body. I loathe my life; I would not live forever. Let me alone for my days are a breath.* — Job 7:11-16

We need to meditate on Rudolph Otto's description of God as *tremendum et fascinans* or the one who both repels and attracts. If we meditated on this God who cannot be reduced to being manageable or predictable, we might be able to recognize another side of God in our transitions. It is this God to whom we now turn our attention. And we do so first by contrasting two words whose use in common parlance gives us a different "feel" for the Mystery we call God: awesome and Godawful.

"Awesome, man, awesome!" Awesome is a word, which we might use to describe the sculpted biceps of an Arnold Schwarzenegger, or a ballerina pirouetting gracefully in Swan Lake, or a lightning storm illuminating the horizon, or the birth of a baby. We greet the awesome with Oohs! and Ahs! and sometimes with silence. Often we would like to share our experience with anyone in shouting distance. Or, absorbed in the experience, we make a mental note to share it later. "Wait til' I tell so and so about this!" The awesome can inspire reverence and evoke an "Oh my god!" regardless of whether we believe in a deity or not.

But these awesome things ought not to be identified so quickly with the awesome itself. A Schwarzenegger or a ballerina are the occasions or vehicles through which we encounter the awesome, but they themselves are not the source of awe. Whether we are drawn to exclaim, "Awesome!" or to notice anything particularly awesome depends on many things. It depends on whether we're disposed to experience what is awesome at this time, in this place, in and through this person, thing, or event. If the ballerina doesn't elicit the awesome response maybe witnessing the birth of a child will do it! The awesome can appear in as many ways as there are creatures in the universe, but no one of them *is* the awesome. If we are not careful the awe which sports figures, religious leaders, and movie stars inspire can easily slip into worship, which only God deserves.

If the awesome inspires and attracts, then the Godawful frightens, frustrates, and often repels. We do not cherish our Godawful experiences the way we do the awesome. Yet, paradoxically, our reflection on some of our transitions might lead us to discover the presence of the awesome in the Godawful. What kinds of experiences could be Godawful? We get caught in a Godawful snowstorm as we travel home from work. Or we're stranded in a Godawful traffic jam. Maybe we've been going through a Godawful divorce, or we're in the middle of a Godawful depression. Perhaps we've been spinning our wheels or have gotten stuck in a rut for months — for no apparent reason. And we feel like we're going crazy. "Godawful!"

Why do we say these times are Godawful? Why not just awful? At the very least they are Godawful because they overwhelm, seem endless, and render us helpless. We could say these experiences are awful but awful doesn't reflect the magnitude of what is happening. What is Godawful about a depression is that it is so disordering and disruptive. We wonder what we've done to deserve what's happening to us. Going through a divorce can be Godawful because the divorce calls into question how we have lived our lives, who we are, and what the future holds. It doesn't seem fair that this should happen to us! A Godawful snowstorm is terrifying because it reminds us how fragile we are. And why of all days should it occur on the only day we have to drive miles for an important appointment? Again, it isn't fair!

But there is more to the Godawful than these unsettling, disruptive, terrifying characteristics. What's God got to do with awful? How could we put God alongside awful and get Godawful? Isn't this blasphemous? Offensive? What makes us so sure that God is only capable of making an appearance in flowing robes with orb and scepter, smiling benignly on grateful subjects but not in our breakups and breakdowns? Why do we not allow God to be in our dark nights of wrestling with belief and unbelief? Can we only meet God, the gentle shepherd, on the holy ground of our churches but not also wherever we confront the overwhelming, unnamable power that shatters our assumptions, overturns what we plan, organize, and arrange for the god of our timetable?

Reflecting on the inadequacy of our concepts to grasp the reality of God, the Jesuit Robert Kennedy writes that even to say God is good is to project our own ideas of goodness onto God. By doing this he believes this is always fatal to our faith:

For indeed when a disaster occurs, we may be scan-
dalized that a "good" God could allow it. With this
mind-set we have good reason to question God's "hu-
man" goodness. We may be tempted to ask what "good"
human being would provide for the world the way God
sometimes does?[1]

And after observing that, Gregory of Nyssa wrote that all we can say of God is that "God is" and that "God is for us," Kennedy comments how sad it is that:

Organized religion domesticates and dwarfs God to a
controllable and loveable size. Influenced as we are by
organized religion, it is no wonder that our prayers can
become a boring struggle to preserve images and analo-
gies that do not serve a mature experience of faith.[2]

If we turn to the book of Jonah, the God who confronts Jonah is for Jonah, Godawful. While Jonah's experience seems removed from ours the reasons that gave rise to his experience are as relevant today as they were when the book was written.

The book of Jonah is only a few pages long. Briefly it is about the prophet Jonah who is ordered by the Lord to go to Nineveh. This was like sending a Londoner to a city much like Berlin during the Third Reich, to proclaim how wicked they were. Not surprisingly, Jonah decides to "flee" from the Lord and go to a place called Tarshish. We are not told why he tries to get away from the Lord. He boards a boat for Tarshish but runs into trouble when the Lord creates a great storm and the boat is in danger of sinking. The mariners are frightened, cry to their god for help, and throw whatever they can overboard to lighten the boat's load. Meanwhile Jonah is fast asleep in the hold of the ship. When the captain discovers Jonah, he begs him to plead with the Lord to spare all on board.

The sailors then cast lots to determine whose fault it is that they are in the middle of a storm. When they discover it is Jonah they ask him who he is, what he does, and where he came from. When he tells them who he is and that he is fleeing from the Lord they are upset. They want to know what they should do. Jonah tells them to throw him into the sea since he is responsible for the storm. Reluctantly they do so only after the storm worsens. A whale soon swallows Jonah where he remains within its belly for three days and nights. Jonah then prays to the Lord for deliverance and the Lord causes the whale to vomit Jonah out on dry land. Once more the Lord orders Jonah to go to Nineveh and announce that the city will be destroyed. In response to this message the Ninevites pray and fast that God will have mercy on them. God changes his mind and decides not to destroy them.

At the end of the story we discover the reason why Jonah fled the Lord in the first place. Jonah says, "For I knew that you are a gracious God and merciful, slow to anger, and abounding in steadfast love, and ready to relent from punishing." Because of God's mercy, Jonah decides he wants to die. But the Lord asks, "Is it right for you to be angry?" Thereupon Jonah goes to the outskirts of the city, makes a booth for himself, and waits to see what will become of the city. At this point it is important for us to quote the final scene of the story since it will be necessary to refer to this incident later.

> *The Lord God appointed a bush, and made it come up over Jonah, to give shade over his head, to save him from his discomfort; so Jonah was very happy about the bush. But when dawn came up the next day, God appointed a worm that attacked the bush, so that it withered. When the sun rose, God prepared a sultry east wind, and the sun beat down on the head of Jonah so that he was faint and asked that he might die. He said, "It is better for me to die than to live."*
>
> *But God said to Jonah, "Is it right for you to be angry about the bush?" And he said, "Yes, angry enough to die." Then the Lord said, "You are concerned about the bush, for which you did not labor and which you did not grow; it came into being in a night and perished in a night. And should I not be concerned about Nineveh, that great city, in which there are more than a hundred and twenty thousand persons who do not know their right hand from their left, and also many animals?"*[3]

Like the transition discussed in chapter 5 this journey story illustrates the necessity of listening to what is happening on both the interpersonal and intrapersonal levels. Jonah attempts to flee the voice of God without. In addition he seems totally oblivious to this voice as it pursues him from within. And when he can no longer ignore God's demands Jonah has a major problem with God's plan. Jonah's spiritual transformation is aborted because he resists the change of heart needed for this to occur.

What gives rise to Jonah's experience of Godawful that can help us in our own experiences of Godawful? As we noted earlier, only at the end of the book do we discover Jonah's reason for avoiding God's command. He feared God would be merciful once the Ninevites repented. Jonah believes and is unyielding in his belief that the Ninevites *deserve* what is coming to them. He fled to Tarshish because, "I knew that you are a gracious God and merciful, slow to anger, and abounding in steadfast love, and ready to relent from punishing." Jonah's problem is that people deserve what happens to them. It's only fair.

Jonah's resistance to God's mercy and forgiveness mirrors how strongly we might react when forgiveness is the issue. We catch people when they say something self-incriminating. "Don't lie to me! I spoke to seven people who saw you there!" Or we catch them in the act and say, "Didn't I tell you — no cookies before dinner!" We catch them cheating, making love, making faces, and all sorts of behaviors. And once we catch them we seldom act kindly toward them. "Let them squirm," we say. We're not going to let them off the hook. They deserve to suffer for what they've done. And if someone says, "I'm sorry," or, "I won't do it again," we're still not going to let him or her off the hook that easily. "Not so fast, Buster. You've got a lot of explaining to do," or, "It doesn't work that way — you can't act as though nothing's happened!" Even if the person acknowledges hurting us and wants to make amends, we aren't going to let the culprit off the hook! We've got him right where we want him, and we intend to keep him there. Like Jonah, we, too, can be unyielding by not forgiving, and insisting that people get what they deserve.

Given Jonah's conviction about the Ninevites deserving punishment, it is no wonder he wanted to flee from God and travel as far as possible in the direction opposite Nineveh. But there is a danger in holding an idea so tenaciously that we aren't open to another's perspective including God's. The danger is polarization not only between others and ourselves but also between our unconscious and ourselves.

In the last chapter we observed that who we are and what we are capable of becoming is much greater than any conscious perspective we might entertain about ourselves. If we become too rigid or overly identified with "my" way of seeing things, then we're no longer available to other inner voices, e.g., intuitions, feelings, or dreams, coming from the deep center which Jung referred to as the Self. In the last chapter we described the Self as the person's core reality. To be true to one's Self is to be true to the Self with an upper case S, not lower case s. In Shakespeare's *Hamlet*, Polonius tells his son Laertes, "To thine own self be true." This is closer to the Self that Jung spoke about. It may also be likened to the *imago dei*, the image of God within. As we have seen it is important that there be some kind of intrapersonal dialogue within the Self to facilitate connection with it. By severing our alliance on the intrapersonal level we set ourselves at odds with the Self. This is what happened to Jonah.

Jonah's one-sided approach, "You get what you deserve" created a conflict within Jonah from the beginning of the story when he fled the voice of God. This is reminiscent of lines from *The Hound of Heaven* by Francis Thompson:

> *I fled Him down the nights and down the days;*
> *I fled Him, down the arches of the years;*
> *I fled Him, down the labyrinthine ways*
> *Of my own mind; and in the mist of tears*
> *I hid from Him, and under running laughter.*
> *Up vistaed hopes, I sped;*
> *And shot, precipitated,*
> *A down Titanic glooms of chasmed fears,*
> *From those strong Feet that followed, followed after,*
> *But with unhurrying chase,*

And unperturbed pace,
Deliberate speed, majestic instancy,
They beat — and a Voice beat
More instant than the Feet —
"All things betray thee, who betrayest Me."[4]

The disturbance *within* Jonah's unconscious is symbolized in the boat's being tossed about like a toy in stormy waters. We read in the story, however, that even in the storm Jonah seemed oblivious and remained asleep in the hold of the ship until the captain woke him, crying, "What are you doing sound asleep? Get up, call on your god! Perhaps the god will spare us a thought so that we do not perish?" In our own single mindedness we can get so caught up in our perspective that we remain blissfully unaware of the stormy waters brewing in the unconscious. But at some point the conflict surfaces and often this happens when someone cares enough to draw our attention to how agitated we are.

Becoming aware of the Godawful storm and how his presence was responsible for endangering the sailors' lives, Jonah jumps overboard and is swallowed by the whale. We might interpret this scene as symbolizing Jonah waking up to the Godawful storm within himself through various symptoms disturbing his conscious life, e.g., anxiety, guilt, and irritability. So intense are these symptoms that they become all-consuming as further symbolized by his being swallowed by the whale. If we fail to do anything about our own conflicts we too might find ourselves in the belly of the whale!

For us the belly of the whale might be those times when we are in a dark mood, very depressed, or highly agitated. Then we might think there is something terribly wrong with us because we are depressed. However since depression is often about loss, it is possible that depression is a symptom of the loss of illusions that we cannot consciously acknowledge, e.g., long held assumptions about life which are now questionable, cherished beliefs about someone that we can't admit are wrong. Our refusal to notice these losses is both a psychological and a spiritual issue. Thus God could be calling to us from within by way of the Self to live our lives with more integrity than we have been doing. To the extent that we avoid listening to the inner reality, we avoid listening to God. "All things betray thee, who betrayest Me." This generates the experience of Godawful.

As we noted in the story of the Good Samaritan, the problem is compounded when assailed by doubts and questions about a perspective that previously seemed unassailable, we project our afflictions onto others whom we see as our enemy. They are threatening and the source of our problem. Godawful envelops us as our world collapses.

Jonah's three-day hold in the whale dramatizes that he cannot evade the call to do God's bidding. So, after the whale had regurgitated him, he marched to Nineveh to preach against the Ninevites. But the problem, which initiated Jonah's flight from God, remained. He preached destruction, the Ninevites repented, and his fear that God would be merciful became a reality. Jonah was furious that God was merciful and he withdrew to the outskirts of the city where he waited to see what would happen. But his experience of Godawful continued as he alternately was comforted by the shade of the bush, and afflicted by the heat of the noonday sun when the tree was destroyed. Jonah was angry and wondered why this had happened. The whole incident was Godawful's way of illustrating how God's mercy is not merited but bestowed freely on whomever God chooses.

But God's position clashed with Jonah's insistence that the Ninevites be punished. They deserved it! So we come back to the fundamental problem, i.e., Jonah's insistence that people should get what they deserve. It is here in the matter of deserving or not deserving that Jonah's problem is also a problem we all face. In order to understand the significance of Jonah's complaint we might recall how important the categories of deserving and undeserving are in interpreting many of our experiences.

Consider a few simple examples of deserving or not deserving. Where would we be if we gave A's to children who didn't deserve A's? Or B's to children who deserved C's? What would happen if we gave gold medals to people who deserved tin pins? Don't we think that people who cheat on their income tax deserve to go to prison? If we're good soldiers or team players don't we deserve a raise? Certainly if we're goldbrickers and slouches on the job we deserve to be fired, don't we? Even if we haven't figured out why we deserve or don't deserve we still subscribe to the theory. "What did I do to deserve this, e.g., heart attack, marital breakup, job loss?" Automatically we assume deserving or not deserving is the way the game is played even if we can't explain the why of it. Do something stupid, and ... you deserve! Do something smart, and ... you deserve!

Why do we think it's got to be this way? Why do we think what happens is a matter of deserving or not deserving? Two reasons come to mind. One is we don't relish thinking that life is one big happening. People who get lung cancer get it because they smoke. And if they never smoked? Well, they breathed in someone else's smoke! And if they rarely got close to another smoker's smoke? Well ... there's got to be an explanation! Somehow they must deserve it.

Another reason we think in terms of deserving or not deserving is our sense of fair play. Where's the justice in this world if a serial killer walks the street a free man? Where's the justice if he doesn't get what's coming to him? Or, nobody but nobody is going to be good to us unless we have done something to deserve it. "Why do you like me? What's your angle? Are you up to something? What's in it for you? C'mon, buddy ... tell the truth! Is it my looks? My charm? The way I part my hair? My bank account?"

Whatever our reasons for holding that deserving or not deserving are the only rules that count, the truth is we've pretty much let these rules govern our lives. No wonder Jonah was upset. Jonah's call to conversion was a call not only to acknowledge his need to be in the right but also to be aware of the inadequacy of projecting categories of deserving/undeserving onto the way in which God ought to be merciful. God's dramatic gesture of providing and then removing the bush was meant to help Jonah get the point. But we do not know if he ever did because the book of Jonah ends with God telling Jonah,

> *"You are concerned about the bush, for which you did
> not labor and which you did not grow; it came into*

being in a night and perished in a night. And should I
not be concerned about Nineveh, that great city, in which
there are more than a hundred and twenty thousand
persons who do not know their right hand from their
left, and also many animals?   — Jonah 4:10-11

Perhaps it is just as well that the book ends with God's question. After all it remains inconclusive whether any of us have really appropriated God's message. Certainly the message met resistance in Jesus' lifetime. Frequently in parables and in his confrontation with religious leaders, he communicated the same message we find in the book of Jonah. The parable of the workers in the vineyard (Matthew 20:1-16) and the Prodigal Son (Luke 15:11-32) illustrate this message. And in Matthew 5:44-45 we read, "But I say to you, love your enemies and pray for those who persecute you, so that you may be children of your Father in heaven; for he makes his sun rise on the evil and on the good, and sends rain on the righteous and on the unrighteous" (cf. also Luke 19:1-10 and Luke 6:35).

It is understandable that like Jonah we might be inclined to evade God's call to be forgiving and refuse to reconsider the way we relate to others on the basis of deserving/undeserving. The reason is we aren't only wrestling with what we might find repugnant, e.g., murderers not getting what they deserve through capital punishment, but we are also wrestling with Godawful whose standards are not our own. Godawful subverts our assumptions by causing us to question and doubt what we have firmly believed for years.

There is, then, a close relationship between the problems Jonah faced and his experience of God as Godawful. In identifying the relationship we are in a better position to understand some of our own experiences of Godawful. Interpreting experience through the categories of deserving/undeserving is one way of orienting ourselves within our world. And even when we can't grasp how deserving/undeserving applies in certain circumstances we assume there must be an explanation along these lines. We think that we simply haven't figured it out yet. "God's ways are not our ways," we say. However, if we lose faith in this interpretive framework not only does our experience of the world change, but so does our experience of God.

In a familiar world God is our trustworthy friend. But when the world becomes a threatening place to live because it no longer makes sense, then God is experienced as "God the Enemy," and God remains the enemy until a new world of meaning emerges. God the Enemy is Godawful, "the heavy" in our lives.

Discovering the inadequacy of a present understanding of our world, and ourselves the problem of taking as ultimate what is preliminary — a truth as The Truth — is a process. It leads us ever deeper into the realization that now we see through a glass darkly as Paul described it. Our journey progressively reveals what we do not know, the learned ignorance of which the mystics speak. In this ignorance we find ourselves comprehended by the incomprehensible Mystery we call God.

Our reflection on Jonah and his encounter with Godawful ought to help clarify what often happens in our transitions. We might be fleeing our own Godawful experiences through a flurry of activities that we hope will help us first ignore and finally forget our experience. We might even pray that God deliver us from what is so terrifying. How ironic that we should pray to God to do away with God's manifestation as Godawful. How urgent the task of discovering that the God we are seeking is the God we are fleeing.

Exercises

1. Think of how you reacted when you felt God let you down but you never permitted yourself to express your feelings to God because they were negative feelings. Can you give yourself permission to write what these feelings were and might still be with you? When this exercise is over do you feel you can read these feelings aloud within the group? Do you feel safe enough to do so?

2. Spend some time reflecting on a time when something unexpected happened to you that was wonderful. How did you feel? Did you spend any time thanking God for what happened? If not, can you write down what your feelings were when the

unexpected happened, and what you might have said to God if you had had the presence of mind to do it?

3. Go back in memory to a time when you were angry or upset because of something that happened when you thought God should have intervened. Later did you realize you had too hastily judged God?

Questions For Discussion

1. Do you ever ask, "What have I done to deserve this?" A heart attack? A bad fall? Do you ask the same question when for no apparent reason everything is going your way? Or do you say, "Where is the justice in the world?" Do you think that "deserve" or "not deserve" are the way the world is supposed to run? Are you covertly upset with God because you can't understand if God is so good how can bad things happen to good people or good things happen to bad people?

2. Do you fear being left speechless about God whom you have been taught to love when what you see happening around doesn't seem to add up to the presence of a loving God? When others are afflicted with some painful illness do you feel uneasy because you cannot console the person with comforting words about God's love? What do you say when that person asks why he or she is going through so much suffering? Does your faith require you to be able to explain what happens as the result of God's will? Or does your faith permit you to say that God is as much or more the Unknowable One as knowable, and always breaking or shattering our image or idea of how God is to be God for us?

---

1. Robert Kennedy, S. J., *Zen Spirit, Christian Spirit* (New York: Continuum, 1999), p. 39.

2. *Ibid.*, p. 40.

3. John Sanford, *Through The Belly Of The Whale* (Kansas City, Missouri: Credence Cassettes, 1987). (I have found Sanford's analysis from a Jungian perspective helpful interpreting this story although my goal is different. I suggest the reader listen to his audiocassettes for a detailed Jungian analysis of the story.)

4. Francis Thompson, *The Hound Of Heaven* (Harrisburg, Pennsylvania: Morehouse Publishing, 1998), pp. 4, 6-7.

Chapter 7

From Losing The Way
To Finding The Way

Objective: To recognize disillusionment in our lives is not only
inevitable but also potentially liberating.

*Now on that same day two of them were going to a
village called Emmaus, about seven miles from Jerusalem, and talking with each other about all these things
that had happened. While they were talking and discussing, Jesus himself came near and went with them,
but their eyes were kept from recognizing him. And he
said to them, "What are you discussing with each other
while you walk along?" They stood still, looking sad.
Then one of them, whose name was Cleopas, answered
him, "Are you the only stranger in Jerusalem who does
not know the things that have taken place there in these
days?" He asked them, "What things?" They replied,
"The things about Jesus of Nazareth, who was a
prophet mighty in deed and word before God and all
the people, and how our chief priests and leaders
handed him over to be condemned to death and cruci-
fied him. But we had hoped that he was the one to re-
deem Israel. Yes, and besides all this, it is now the third
day since these things took place. Moreover, some
women of our group astounded us. They were at the
tomb early this morning, and when they did not find
his body there, they came back and told us that they
had indeed seen a vision of angels who said that he
was alive. Some of those who were with us went to the
tomb and found it just as the women had said; but they
did not see him." Then he said to them, "Oh, how foolish you are, and how slow of heart to believe all that
the prophets have declared! Was it not necessary that
the Messiah should suffer these things and then enter
into his glory?" Then beginning with Moses and all*

the prophets, he interpreted to them the things about himself in all the scriptures.

As they came near the village to which they were going, he walked ahead as if he were going on. But they urged him strongly, saying, "Stay with us, because it is almost evening and the day is now nearly over." So he went in to stay with them. When he was at the table with them, he took break, blessed and broke it, and gave it to them. Then their eyes were opened, and they recognized him; and he vanished from their sight. They said to each other, "Were not our hearts burning within us while he was talking to us on the road, while he was opening the scriptures to us?"

That same hour they got up and returned to Jerusalem; and they found the eleven and their companions gathered together. They were saying, "The Lord has risen indeed, and he has appeared to Simon!" They told what had happened on the road, and how had been made known to them in the breaking of he bread.

— Luke 24:13-27

In chapter 2, we observed the captivating power of illusions and how transitions are occasions for liberating us from the illusions of what makes us special. We concluded that we are loved not because we are special, but we are special because God loves us. What we left unexamined in that chapter were our reactions to the disillusionments that attend our transitions, and especially how these reactions can deepen our understanding of God's love for us in surprising ways. That is the focus of this chapter.

Like the story of the Prodigal Son, the Emmaus story is about setting out on a journey and returning with a new perspective. However, unlike the Prodigal's journey, this one is not about leaving home and returning home but one of going home and leaving home. Disillusioned by what had happened to Jesus, his followers abandoned the "Jesus Way" and left Jerusalem. Returning to Emmaus, they underwent a conversion that enabled them to embrace the "Jesus Way" by going back to Jerusalem. What truth did they discover about this "Way" on their journey?

A number of years ago I wrote a little story about Cleopas, the only disciple named in this biblical story. Although I present it as an imaginative sketch of his life because I think it helps us focus on the positive contribution of disillusionment in times of transition.

Broken Promise

"Life is a broken promise now that Jesus is dead," Cleo complained to his friend Eli as they walked on the road to Emmaus. "What's there to live for? Now everything has fallen apart."

Twenty-five years earlier, Cleo had had such high hopes. "My future's promising," he had boasted. "It's looking great! I'm going to find me a good-looking gal. We'll get married, settle down, and have bright kids who'll really go places. I'll own a business that will make me a mint." A promising future? That's what he thought twenty-five years ago. But now at age forty-five, it was a different story.

Cleo had gotten married but not to the girl of his dreams. True, she had pale blue eyes, ruby lips, and a winning smile but she also had a nose bent just slightly to the left. She cooked a good meal; but she couldn't sew a button on a shirt if her life depended on it. She had a good ear for listening but she wasn't much for talking. Humming was her long suit but she sang with a twang.

As for their marriage, sometimes they'd chirp along but just as often they'd growl. Smiling one day, they snarled the next. All in all the marriage wasn't bad but Cleo had had such high hopes — and now life seemed a broken promise.

And his children? The kids who'd eagerly listen to mom and dad's words of wisdom? The bright kids who were really going places? One was smart in math but dumb in spelling; the other was smart in spelling but dumb in math. They weren't bad looking but they had their mother's nose which bent just slightly to the left.

119

As for listening to their parents' words of advice, they listened all right. Then they'd scratch their heads, shrug their shoulders and do whatever they wanted. Both of them moved to the other side of town and worked in the local glue factory. It didn't take much to make them happy. Cleo had had such high hopes for them and now life seemed a broken promise.

And the promising career? Cleo owned and operated a bagel bakery. Not the smallest business in town but not the biggest. His bagels weren't bad, but they weren't the best either. He made money but not the mint he said he'd make. All in all, his was a modestly successful business. Cleo had had such high hopes and now life was passing by. It seemed a broken promise.

As if to prove that "There's no fool like an old fool," well into his forties Cleo got suckered in again. This time he pinned his high hopes on Jesus of Nazareth. "Surely he won't let me down," Cleo thought. "Jesus is the one. He's the wave of the future. He's our promise. A real winner here! His power base is here and he's going to drive the bully boys away. He'll make this a land of promise again and we'll be on the move." But the promised one was nailed to the tree and left to die a broken man. Hardly a winner and no one's future. Just another broken promise. And for Cleo, the last straw.

"I just don't understand," Cleo complained as he and his friend Eli walked the dusty road to Emmaus. "What went wrong? He wasn't supposed to die. That wasn't in the cards. Where's the winner we were promised? I'll tell you ... nowhere! Sure, a couple of women report he's alive but that's absurd, impossible!"

"May I join you?"

"Wha...?"

Cleo and Eli turned to see a man walking a few feet behind.

"May I join you? I don't like walking this road alone."

"Suit yourself," Cleo said. "We were just talking about Jesus of Nazareth."

"Oh? What about him?"

"You mean you haven't heard the news?"

"I've been away for three days."

"Well, he's not what we'd thought. Just another flash in the pan, another broken promise." Cleo proceeded to tell the man all that had happened not only to Jesus, but all the disappointments in his own life as well.

"Hmmm," the man stroked his chin. "Your story sounds vaguely familiar. About three years ago I was convinced that all of us: my friends, the people I talked to, myself—that we all had a promising future. Changes in our lives were to take place over night. The day would dawn when people from all over would sit around one table and enjoy each other's company. We knew we'd have to overcome certain obstacles. But we'd win out! We'd triumph! Life seemed so promising!" The stranger paused.

"And?" Cleo waved a hand.

"Well ... not everyone shared our enthusiasm. In fact, some people were downright hostile! Even the friends we counted on most betrayed us." His voice grew raspy. "And worst of all, the one whose support and love I relied on most seemed to have abandoned me when I needed him most!"

"Really?" Both Cleo and Eli's eyes widened.

"Yes, when I was just hanging there, hurting, I said, 'Where are you when I need you?' And, you know, he said nothing. Nothing!"

"No kidding! So what did you do?" Eli asked.

"At first I thought 'That's it! There goes the future! Promises, promises! Right out the window!' I felt wretched and in a lot of pain. But then I thought 'So there's a change of plans. So it's not working out according to my expectations! I can't do anything about that. I'll just hang in there, wait, and trust it will all work out. What else can I do?'"

"And what happened?"

"I think I died."

"I know the feeling well," Cleo sighed.

"You what?" Eli was all in a muddle.

"I think I died," the stranger repeated, looking off into the distance.

"But ... you're here. How...?"

"I'm here but ... all I know is that the one whom I thought had abandoned me, pulled me through. And now I'm alive in a new way. Even my friends aren't going to recognize me right away. It's a changed ball game, believe me! Just when you think 'It's over. My life is just a heap of broken promises....' Surprise! Back alive in a way no one expected!"

"Hmmm, I never thought of it that way," Cleo said. Turning to the man he asked, "Have we met before? Your voice ... your smile...."

"Maybe I resemble someone you know."

"Could be. Could be," Cleo said, trying without success to recall who this engaging young man resembled. However they had reached Emmaus and the stranger told them he had to continue on his way. But Cleo and Eli persuaded him to join them at the bagel factory for a light lunch.

When they arrived, Cleo spread a white tablecloth over a work bench and placed on it a small loaf of bread, a carafe of wine, and three goblets. Once they sat down Cleo invited the stranger to do the honor of breaking the bread.

Taking the bread into his hands, the man ran his fingers over the small loaf. "Nice texture! Did you bake it?"

"Yes," Cleo answered. "This morning."

"Ah, freshly risen," he whispered, "and it smells so good." No sooner had the stranger spoken the word "risen" than Cleo's heart began beating faster. He remembered the stranger's words about coming alive in a new way and it struck Cleo how closely this man's experience paralleled Jesus' — his hopes, his betrayal, his death, and now? Both Cleo and Eli's eyes were riveted on their guest as he broke the bread and shared the cup.

122

> When they had finished the meal the man said, "We
> know each other better now, don't we? I hope you will
> remember me whenever you break bread together."
> "Yes," Cleo said softly. "We will."
> The stranger rose. "It's time for me to go. I have
> much to do. I have many friends with whom I'll be break-
> ing bread. Thank you for your hospitality. Please stay
> sitting. I'll let myself out." And the man left the house.
> "It's him," Cleo whispered.
> "I know," Eli said.
> Cleo rose, went to the window, and watched the
> stranger as he disappeared over the horizon. "He's
> come back, Eli. He's come back!"[1]

This story highlights two sets of expectations, those of Cleo and those of Jesus. It also suggests a resolution to the crisis engendered by unmet expectations. Like most of us, Cleo had high expectations early in his life. His wife, children, and career would be everything he imagined them to be. But as he grew older what he expected didn't occur. Life seemed like a succession of broken promises. He had expected more from his wife, children, or job than they could possibly deliver.

Cleo's experience of broken promises continued with Jesus and how Cleo expected he would save his people. He had imagined Jesus as the leader who would drive the Romans out of Israel. But like his earlier expectations these weren't met either. In answer to his own question, "Where's the winner we were promised?" he reacted, "I'll tell you ... nowhere!" Cleo felt cheated. Although Cleo didn't react to his feeling of betrayal in all the same ways we might have, identifying some of them gives us an idea of how devastating disillusionment can be.

Reactions In Disillusionment[2]

Disillusionment often has this effect: If we had idealized a person, ideology, or institution we might now demonize it. We find fault with everything about it. What we once heralded as beautiful, noble, and good, we now regard as ugly, ignoble, and bad. We wonder how we were ever so blinded by what is now so obviously unacceptable. Cleo was disillusioned by Jesus' failure to be the winner Cleo expected, and he bitterly concluded that Jesus was nowhere to be found.

But Cleo was also upset with himself for having placed his hope in Jesus. In other words, Cleo not only felt let down by Jesus, he had also let himself down. "How could I be so stupid? Why was I so blind? What was I thinking?" This is *self-rejection*. When in hindsight we see ourselves as having been naive, or gullible, we belittle the side of ourselves that was trusting and open. We prefer disowning the vulnerable side of ourselves to owning ourselves where we are hurting most. This reaction is potentially crippling since it can prevent us from entrusting ourselves to others if it may mean getting hurt again.

Betrayal might also make us *cynical*. Having been disillusioned with this woman, or man, or institution we generalize that all women, or men, or institutions can't be trusted. "When you've seen one, you've seen them all! They're all looking out for their own good! It's a dog-eat-dog world!" Sometimes we mask our cynicism through religious statements, e.g., we can trust only God. But this is simply another way of saying we can't trust anybody. Others might let us down but God won't. We don't realize how we also feel rejected by God when God doesn't answer a prayer or respond to a need that we expect God to meet. Since we might have been trained not to question God's ways our resentment gets buried beneath protestations of how God is the only one whom we can trust.

Our negative reactions are understandable and perhaps necessary if we are to be realistic about what we had idealized or idolized. They are the withdrawal pains that come from detaching ourselves from our attachments. They are also the initial phase of being liberated from what had captivated our minds and hearts.

Of course there is a danger that we might not get beyond these initial reactions and consequently fail to reinvest our energies in creative ways. Cynicism and self-rejection can consume us. Or we might reinvest all our energies in yet another relationship, or project, or ideology, and once more become overly attached. However if we can appreciate our reactions as withdrawal pains in a healing journey of being liberated from destructive attachments, then we might find meaning in our pain. Cleo's journey to Emmaus was this kind of a journey. But the deeper meaning of Cleo's journey emerges when we see how his disillusionment connects to Jesus' own experience of dying and rising.

Hanging In There

In "Broken Promise" we imagine Jesus' reflections of his own experience. He told Cleo and Eli, "When I was just hanging there, hurting, I said, 'Where are you when I need you?' And you know, he said nothing. Nothing!" At first Jesus reacted as Cleo had. "Promises, promises! Right out the window!" But gradually without understanding what was happening he accepted the change in plans. All he could do was "hang in there, wait, and trust it will all work out." The key to understanding Jesus' response to his own disillusionment is the significance of "hanging in there."

"Hanging in there" expresses how we are getting along, handling a job, working through a relationship, doing in school, and so on. During these times hanging in there is not particularly difficult. We're pretty confident that we'll do all right; we'll manage. However, at other times hanging in there means being painfully helpless. We're not sure how we'll survive a difficult time, e.g., a midlife transition or the loss of a loved one. The pain of hanging in there reveals just how broken we are in body, mind, and spirit.

These times of hanging in there are frequently dark and depressing, hardly times we'd expect to survive. Yet, as our story suggests, hanging in there can also mean trusting and waiting. We wait and wait. For what? For something new to develop. For a breakthrough. For transformation. For new life. For us trusting and waiting don't mean that after a period of hanging in there we finally figure a way out. It means we have reached an impasse and cannot find any way to stop hanging in there. All we can do is trust that as in Jesus' hanging and dying God will also be with us.

Hanging in there is both a sign of our being helpless and the medium through which we can be transformed from death to life. This happens not because it has to but because we believe the one who raised Jesus from the dead has promised it will happen. As the medium of transformation, hanging in there leads us from darkness into light. Initially, we do not see a way out of our predicament, and because we are blind we wait in the dark to "see" in a new way. Seeing in a new way is intimately connected with the purification of our illusions. We have our illusions concerning how God is to be God for us. But how God is to be God is not up to us. It is up to God. This necessarily means the shattering of our illusions about how God will be God for us and the direction our lives are to move us. "The change of plans" to which Jesus refers in the story was his way of acknowledging he had to die to his own preconceived idea of how his life would be played out.

It was Jesus' passion and death that prevented Cleo and his friend from recognizing Jesus on the road to Emmaus. In the biblical story of Emmaus, "to recognize" (Greek: *epiginosko*) refers to knowing Jesus personally. This kind of knowing is different from knowing the truth of a message. As LaVerdiere puts it, Jesus' disciples would not be able to recognize him until they could personally face the passion with him and enter into its mystery. They needed to reflect on all of the scriptures:

> to understand that as the Christ he had to suffer the passion and enter into his glory (24:26). Taught by the Lord Jesus what it meant for him to be prophet and Christ, the disciples were now prepared to know and recognize him in the breaking of the bread.[3]

"What it meant for him" was Jesus' passion and death. What it came to mean for Jesus is a way of stating that Jesus' understanding of his passage (passion and death) was a process of the purification of his illusions about what the future held for him.

Hospitality

With hearts burning within them, Jesus' disciples were prepared to recognize him in the breaking of the bread as they asked him, "Stay with us" (Greek: *meno*). The Greek verb is of special significance in Luke's Gospel. It means, "to dwell." When Luke uses it "it refers to making one's home with others and dwelling with them ... For Luke the church is a place of hospitality, a welcoming home, and Christians are people who make their home in and with one another."[4] The disciples offered this stranger hospitality and that included sharing a meal together. It was only when he had shared his person with them, and they reciprocated by breaking bread with him, that they recognized him as Lord.

It is important that we understand the disciples' recognition of Jesus as Lord depended on their entering the mystery of his passion and their hospitality through breaking bread with him. We have dwelt on the purification of illusions through hanging in there as a means of "seeing" in a new way. What is its connection with hospitality? In the process of being purified of illusions we become progressively aware of how we have seen the other (others, God, life) in terms of our own needs. Seeing the other from the perspective of our needs distorts the other's reality. Consequently, our being available to the other is a conditioned hospitality, but genuine hospitality means being available to the other as other, and not as filtered through our needs. By being themselves, people who are hospitable enable us to feel at home and be ourselves. We do not need to pretend or put on airs to be who or what our host needs us to be. When Jesus breaks bread at Emmaus, he takes on the role of the host in the home of the host. *He* breaks bread! The disciples and Jesus are mutually available, giving and receiving.

This idea of hospitality prepares the disciples for recognizing who it is that is breaking bread. Why? Being hospitable enables us to reach out to others beyond our preconceptions and biases so that they can be themselves. We do not demand that they be more or less than they are. The progressive purification of illusions throughout our lives potentially liberates us to be hospitable wherever we are whether in others' homes or our own. The paradox is that as we exercise hospitality by not requiring people be more than they are, our hospitality disposes them to disclose more than we dreamt they could be. Just so, being hospitable enabled the disciples to take the final step in recognizing the Risen Lord in the breaking of the bread.

Jesus could be the Risen Lord only when the disciples, purified of their illusions of how Jesus had to be Lord, received him in their midst as he was. Then he was free to be more than he appeared to be. We can extend this insight to our understanding of the Christian community as the Body of Christ.

Being hospitable means being available to others as they are and not to what we need them to be. But what they are capable of being is precisely what the story of the empty tomb and Jesus' resurrection suggests. Since Jesus was no longer limited to a particular time and place he could become available as the Risen Lord in the breaking of the bread, and in the community of believers.

But we ought not to interpret this to mean that we "try to see Christ in others" when we are exercising hospitality. No. We do not "need" to see Jesus in anybody. We want to welcome others as they are. Maybe then we might make the surprising discovery that they and we are more than we are, i.e., Something Else, the Body of Christ. Like the disciples' journey, ours, too, is necessarily one of disillusionment, of hospitality, and finally of recognizing the Risen Lord not only in the breaking of the bread but however he chooses to be present.

"Returning to Jerusalem" is a way of speaking about a clearer vision of what one is called to do and be in life. Through their journey the disciples arrived at a better understanding of who they were, who Jesus was, and what they were called to do. Hopefully many of us achieve greater clarity about who we are vis-à-vis ourselves, the world, and God. But greater clarity does not mean our journeys are over. These continue. We are always in need of conversion. Jerusalem might be the disciples' destination but it is also their point of departure for new horizons. Our transitions might open up new horizons but no one transition constitutes the last horizon. As long as we walk on this earth we are forever on the Way.

Exercises

1. Spend some time identifying a time when you felt let down by a friend, a spouse, or a religious institution. How deeply involved were you with the person or institution that let you down? Write in your notebook what was disillusioning and the feelings this experience generated. How did you deal with your sense of betrayal? Did you in any way suspect that what happened would happen but you couldn't admit it to yourself?

2. Is it possible that something positive can emerge out of these painful experiences of disillusionment? After going through a period of disillusionment do you think you are less likely to invest your energies in anyone or anything as you had prior to the disillusionment? Do you think being so completely captivated by a person or thing can become addictive and that being disillusioned possibly helps release you from that illusion?

3. Have you ever let someone down? Did you feel it necessary because the person was becoming too attached to you? Or too dependent? Had you in any way encouraged the other to become attached or dependent in covert ways? If you had to disillusion the person was there any way you could have done it gently, or is it even possible to disillusion someone without that person suffering from the disillusionment? Are there times when we need to disillusion someone, e.g., someone has an inflated idea of his or her or your abilities and needs to be confronted on this?

Questions For Discussion

1. When Jesus was on the cross just "hangin' in there" in the story "Broken Promises," how do you interpret this as his way of dealing with his sense of abandonment by God? Can the expression be understood in different ways? Can we speak of hanging in there when we mean just holding on for dear life,

129

or can we also mean we trust God will be there and this hanging is a time of transformation. The transforming experience is the liminal or in-between time in a transition when often hanging in there is all we can do.

2.   When you go through an experience of disillusionment regarding your faith what does this reveal about your relationship with God? Do you say, "I'm in the dark! I don't know what's happening!" Is being in the dark like being in a cocoon or going into hibernation for a while? Could being in the dark mean that you need to die to one way of understanding God if you are to achieve a deeper understanding? Being in the dark is what the mystics refer to as the dark night when we are purified of our illusions about God. Could you think of this experience as resembling a new understanding of an old friend? In other words when your usually happy-go-lucky friend breaks down and reveals something about himself totally out of character wouldn't you feel lost for a while about how to relate to him? Wouldn't you be in the dark before you arrived at a new way of relating to him? Doesn't this experience tell you something about your developing relationship with God?

---

1. Andre Papineau, "Broken Promise," *Lightly Goes The Good News* (Lima, Ohio: CSS Publishing Company Inc., 2002), pp. 180-184.

2. I am indebted to James Hillman's essay, "Betrayal," *Loose Ends* (New York: Spring Publications, 1995), where a fuller explanation of these reactions can be found.

3. Eugene LaVerdiere, *Dining In The Kingdom Of God* (Chicago: Liturgy Training Publications, 1994), p. 167.

4. *Ibid.*, p. 168.

Chapter 8

From Well Water
To Living Water

Objective: To identify our human experiences as potentially revelatory of the sacred in our lives.

Now when Jesus learned that the Pharisees had heard, "Jesus is making and baptizing more disciples than John" — although it was not Jesus himself but his disciples who baptized — he left Judea and started back to Galilee. But he had to go through Samaria. So he came to a Samaritan city called Sychar, near the plot of ground that Jacob had given to his son Joseph. Jacob's well was there, and Jesus, tired out by his journey, was sitting by the well. It was about noon.

A Samaritan woman came to draw water, and Jesus said to her, "Give me a drink." (His disciples had gone to the city to buy food.) The Samaritan woman said to him, "How is it that you, a Jew, ask a drink of me, a woman of Samaria?" (Jews do not share things in common with Samaritans.) Jesus answered her, "If you knew the gift of God, and who it is that is saying to you, 'Give me a drink,' you would have asked him, and he would have given you living water." The woman said to him, "Sir, you have no bucket, and the well is deep. Where do you get that living water? Are you greater than our ancestor Jacob, who gave us the well, and with his sons and his flocks drank from it?" Jesus said to her, "Everyone who drinks of this water will be thirsty again, but those who drink of the water that I will give them will never be thirsty. The water that I will give will become in them a spring gushing up to eternal life." The woman said to him, "Sir, give me this water, so that I may never be thirsty or have to keep coming here to draw water."

Jesus said to her, "Go, call your husband, and come back." The woman answered him, "I have no husband."

Jesus said to her, "You are right in saying, 'I have no husband'; for you have had five husbands, and the one you have now is not your husband. What you have said is true!" The woman said to him, "Sir, I see that you are a prophet. Our ancestors worshiped on this mountain, but you say that the place where people must worship is in Jerusalem." Jesus said to her, "Woman, believe me, the hour is coming when you will worship the Father neither on this mountain nor in Jerusalem. You worship what you do not know; we worship what we know, for salvation is from the Jews. But the hour is coming, and is now here, when the true worshipers will worship the Father in spirit and truth, for the Father seeks such as these to worship him. God is spirit, and those who worship him must worship in spirit and truth." The woman said to him, "I know that Messiah is coming" (who is called Christ). "When he comes, he will proclaim all things to us." Jesus said to her, "I am he, the one who is speaking to you."

Just then his disciples came. They were astonished that he was speaking with a woman, but no one said, "What do you want?" or, "Why are you speaking with her?" Then the woman left her water jar and went back to the city. She said to the people, "Come and see a man who told me everything I have ever done! He cannot be the Messiah, can he?" They left the city and were on their way to him. — John 4:1-30

In previous chapters we have described the experiences of set ups and let downs or illusions and disillusionments in transitions as well as societal constructions determining who is in and who is out in biblical and contemporary societies. In this chapter we shall revisit these themes by focusing on the biblical story of the woman at the well. They will be helpful in understanding the fundamental longing this woman and every person has, namely, the yearning for the infinite symbolized as living water in this story.

It is important to preface this reflection on the journey of the Samaritan woman by stating clearly the assumption that governs this chapter. In John's Gospel, the story of the woman is an important episode in the woman's life as she realizes that the water, which will forever quench her thirst, is not the water she has been drawing from the well but the life giving water, which Jesus offers. But there is more to this story than the episode at the well. Her story is a journey that has a history which precedes her meeting Jesus. True, we know little of her past from the gospel but what we know tells us something about the kind of life she led prior to meeting Jesus. The assumption here is that her journey as well as ours are ultimately stories of longing or thirsting for that which satisfies completely, namely the infinite reality we call God. I hope to offer some explanation on both psychological and spiritual grounds for this longing, but I realize that any thorough explanation would require more space than I can give here. All I can do is appeal to our experience as the basis for the assumption that we are all yearning for the infinite despite alternate interpretations of these experiences that others might offer.

Background[1]

She had five husbands and was living with another man. While not all scholars agree she was married and divorced five times,[2] arguably this is what happened. When Jesus met her she would have been considered damaged goods. From a Jewish perspective not only was she unclean because of her lifestyle but also because she was a Samaritan. We have already seen how Jews felt about Samaritans in chapter 5. Moreover, besides being unacceptable among Jews she was a pariah among Samaritans. She came to the well by herself at noon. Usually when a woman came to the well (a public place) to draw water she was accompanied by other women in the cool of early morning or evening. Coming alone, this woman most likely was shunned by the other women. She was an outsider among her own people. Beyond her status within her society we have little information about her. However, we are free to imagine this woman's life by describing what it must have been like to have suffered through so many failed marriages. Considering these failures we can continue imagining what led to her transforming moment at the well. Shortly what follows is a story about what this woman's life might have been like with the men she married.

Longing For The Infinite

Obviously her journey was a journey in which she longed for fulfillment. Given the information we have from the biblical story we might describe her as one who hoped to satisfy her thirst through marital relationships. But again the underlying assumption is that what she and we have in common is our fundamental thirst for what satisfies completely, the infinite. Whether or not we recognize this as the thrust of our longing doesn't diminish its thrust. As Saint Augustine said centuries ago, "Our heart is restless until it rests in thee."[3]

I take this to mean that we are always reaching for the infinite however unaware we might be of what we are reaching for. Yet invariably as we reach for the infinite we end up with the finite. Our reach is always greater than our grasp. Or using the imagery from the gospel we thirst for living water, but end up with water that ultimately doesn't satisfy. Our frustrations result from our unmet expectations to see **It** (God, the infinite) in **it** (the finite, created reality). The heart seeks to rest in whatever seems to offer the possibility of total fulfillment, and in return the heart invests the object of its hope with infinite value. Depending how we interpret our longing we shall either conclude that nothing less than the infinite is ultimately satisfying, or conclude as did the philosopher Jean Paul Sartre that "man is a useless passion," always struggling to be fulfilled but faced finally with an eternal void, nothing.

If we believe that our longing is for the infinite, and that invariably we end up grasping for less than the infinite, we shall also realize that disillusionment of one kind or another is inevitable because no person and no thing can be ultimately satisfying. Disillusionment and the various reactions to this experience I have already described in chapter 7. Here, however, in this story I shall try to be more concrete as we explore this woman's journey of disillusionment as repeatedly she seeks to find **It** and ends up with **it** until she encounters Jesus who turns her life around.

Well, Well, Well

It was noon. And there was no one around to harass her as she left her house and walked down the empty streets. "A has been! Nothing left," she thought as she walked slowly to the well. Then she laughed. "A has been? I've never been anything to begin with.

"What do I mean? A has been!" That summed up her "life" as far as she was concerned. "And those husbands," she sighed. How could she have thought any of them seriously loved her? They were interested in anything but her. She certainly wasn't a beauty queen now or nor had she been when she married her first husband. Other women might have attracted men because of their beauty or charm. But not her. She was appealing to him because of her family's wealth. He knew her dowry would be substantial. So he passionately professed his love for her. But it was her money he had fallen in love with. As to his other love, he was a philanderer who used her money to satisfy his sexual conquests for other women. However, he wasn't very tactful because he bragged of his affairs to others when he had too much to drink. It was only a matter of time before she found out and that was the end of that marriage.

Her second marriage couldn't have been because of her money. Her first husband had taken care of that. There was little left after he had spent so much of it on other women. No, the reason she remarried is the reason so many marry. Both were recently divorced. Both were lonely and needy. They thought by marrying they'd fill the void in their lives. Later she knew they ought to have known better. She realized they must have known in their hearts that marrying one another to fill this void wouldn't work. But they went ahead and married anyway. For a while the marriage seemed to work since

*they always felt the need to be in one another's pres-
ence. But gradually they discovered their need was
mutually smothering since they placed demands on each
other that neither could meet. The pressures increased
and so, too, did the need to distance themselves from
one another — permanently. Whatever love had been
present died when they realized what they were doing
to one another.*

*And number three? Why a third marriage? She
wasn't sure. She thought maybe she had learned from
her mistakes. Or had she become less and less concerned about making them? "Who knows? It could
work!" she thought. Marrying became easier but remaining married was no longer a sure thing. After all,
past track records have a way of influencing the future.
And failed marriages undermined her trust that she
could succeed with this husband. These failures haunted
her as she tried working through the problems in her
third marriage. However, not only did she feel she was
failing but she blamed herself for her husband's failures. "It's not his fault," she told a friend. "It's mine.
I've done what I've always done ... mess things up!"
She felt terribly guilty and her husband couldn't help
her. He could only help himself. He wanted out. And
that ended number three.*

*One would think she wouldn't marry again. Why
ask for more suffering? Yet in spite of feeling guilty over
failed marriages she still longed to be fulfilled by marrying again. Driven by this thirst she sought out anyone who offered the slightest chance of satisfying it.
Desperate, in the marriages which followed she settled
for men who used and abused her. By the time she married her fifth husband she felt like damaged goods.
Bruised and bloated from booze, she cared little how
others thought of her — except that she didn't want to
be known as a slut. But the men who married her to
satisfy their lust confirmed what she feared.*

*And now that she had left her fifth husband she
had good reason to think of herself as a slut. She had
recently taken up living with a man who was not her
husband.*

136

As she reached the well she thought, "A slut! Has it come to this?" She winced at the thought of it. Pre-occupied with her thoughts, she hadn't noticed the man standing next to her at the edge of the well.

"Could you give me a drink of water?" he asked.

Startled, she looked up at the stranger. "What did you say?"

"I said could you give me a drink of water?"

"Here we go again," she thought. "Coming on to me this way!" She wanted to tell him that she was al-ready spoken for. Another man already occupying her bed at home. He'd have to wait his turn. But she was also intrigued by this man. She could tell by his accent that he wasn't a Samaritan. He was a Jew. That was a twist. A Jew. An enemy. She thought he must have been desperate or sensed that she was desperate. It didn't matter. "You a Jew asking me, a Samaritan, for some water?" She laughed. "You do know where you are, don't you? This is a Samaritan village and you're talk-ing to a Samaritan woman."

"I know. I know. But when you're thirsty, you're thirsty, and if you're desperate you'll go through five husbands to satisfy your thirst."

"What? Are you talking about me?" she asked defensively.

"About being thirsty or about the five husbands?" he asked innocently.

"About being thirsty of course!" she shot back. But she knew it was as much about the husbands as it was about the thirst. "What's your angle?" she demanded.

"My angle? I don't have an angle!"

Didn't he? She wasn't convinced he didn't. But she thought it best to give him what he wanted. "Okay, Okay, I'll draw some water for you if that's all you want." And the woman slowly began to lower her bucket into the water. But as she did he said quietly, "Well there is something else!"

"Ah!" she thought. "Here we go! Yes?" she asked warily as she stopped lowering the bucket.

137

"That water down there. It's like everything else we thirst for. It never satisfies once and for all, does it?" She said nothing. He had hit home.

He continued, "Maybe there's water in another well that satisfies completely."

"Oh!" she shot back. "Another well? This is the only one I know about!"

"The water I'm talking about is inside you."

"Inside me?"

"Yes, inside you! Ready to bubble up and over parched land just like this!" he cried as he stretched his arms and hands towards the desert.

There are times when someone's word taps into painful feelings — feelings of shame and guilt dwelling deep within. The stranger, a Jew no less, offered her the word that tapped into that well deep within. Slowly tears formed in her eyes, then the tears flowed freely, and she sobbed uncontrollably. And the stranger simply sat on the edge of the well. The only words he spoke were, "It's okay! Let it flow! Let it flow!"

And so she did. Not only did her tears flow but so too did her words of failure, despair, self-loathing, guilt, and shame. He continued listening to her story as she spoke of how miserably she had failed in all her marriages. "Five, if I'm not mistaken," he whispered.

"Why yes," she answered. But now she freely admitted what a minute earlier she couldn't acknowledge. Was it because in opening the floodgates of her past he didn't judge her? He listened and didn't judge, and as he listened she felt at peace with herself for the first time in years.

So at peace did she feel that she wanted to tell others how she felt and how this stranger at the well had helped her. Helped her? But how could she explain? That a Jew offered water which would bubble up within? That she told him everything about herself and he didn't judge her? That he knew more about her than she had told him? That what mattered more than anything was that he was there to listen? In her mind it didn't seem to make much sense but still she felt the need to testify

138

what happened at the well. "Sir, I have to go now. But I'll be back. Don't leave! There are others, many others who'll want to hear about this water bubbling up!"

The stranger smiled. "I'll be here. I'll be here."

And she left to tell the villagers about the water in the well — that made her well.[4]

The Distance Between *it* And *It*

" 'A has been! Nothing left,' she thought as she walked slowly to the well. Then she laughed. 'A has been? I've never been anything to begin with. What do I mean? A has been!' That summed up her 'life' as far as she was concerned."

On her way to the well the woman reflects on her life and the marriages she has gone through to achieve fulfillment. Her reaction is self-rejection. She laughs as if she didn't care that all of her marriages collapsed. Self-rejection isn't an uncommon reaction for anyone who has risked being vulnerable and suffered rejection from a friend, lover, or spouse. For the Samaritan woman it is a way of distancing herself from the pain she suffers as a result of her husband taking advantage of her. In this way she hopes to anesthetize the pain. Whatever feelings of anger and hurt she has, she walls off through self-rejection.

Yet, she can't help reviewing her previous marriages as if she sought to trace whatever it was that prompted her to marry, divorce, and remarry so many times. In her first marriage she realizes she was naïve when she married a man who loved her money more than he loved her. While she had been self-disclosing and affectionate, her husband was betraying her. If she had longed to be fulfilled, she sadly realized it wouldn't be with this man. She might have concluded that since she wasn't "a beauty queen and never had been," her longing could never be satisfied. But could she deny this longing? Hardly. However disastrous her first marriage, she couldn't deny her thirst. Like all of us she continued to reach for **It** without realizing **It** would be beyond her grasp as she ended up with **it**. So she marries a second time.

139

In her intense longing to be satisfied, her second husband becomes the misplaced be all and end all of her attraction. Let us assume that the man she married had also been divorced. Following the first divorce both of them were lonely. Expectations were high that each find their needs met in the other. Often a person going through a divorce is hungry for affection and assurances that someone come along and affirms the person as loveable. Many newly-divorced people experience urgency in longing to be loved. Why is this?

They suffer from a loss of self-esteem since they have suffered the loss of the love object in the divorce whether in the death throes of their marriage, or during the in-between time (the liminal space) when they are no longer married. They also experience a quasi-loss of identity since they are no longer the wife or husband of the married partner, nor do they enjoy the network of friends created through their married life. The loss of a partner can be devastating especially if one of the partners had been overly dependent on the other for a sense of well-being and/or identity. In the absence of well-being the desperate desire to be loved prompts the needy person to seek another's love to fill the void. But on a deeper level the intensity of the longing for fulfillment leads one (albeit unwittingly) to marry and demand that the new partner be god. Becoming god for the Samaritan woman means expecting that her new husband be her salvation. But this dynamic might also be taking place in his life. She is there to be his goddess who will save him from his loneliness. Investing one another with expectations neither can meet, their demands go unmet. At some point, their failure to be what each needs the other to be becomes apparent and they separate.

The intense longing for complete fulfillment suggests that the underlying attraction is the infinite. That toward which they are ineluctably drawn (the infinite) is also the very condition for the possibility of loving anyone (the finite). But what is finite shouldn't be understood as insignificant. On the contrary, what is finite is itself an echo of the infinite, and like any echo has it source in the voice without which the echo would have no reality of its own. We are all echoes of the infinite and our reality is not diminished in being echoes. But our reality itself ought to be understood as derivative or coming from the source which is the infinite. What this means is that when two people are drawn to one another whether needy or not they are drawn outside of themselves by God who is always drawing them outside of themselves toward God's Self. That we find ourselves entering into finite relationships through the attraction toward the infinite is God's way of drawing us to God in and through these loving relationships. That we might end up demanding that any one of these relationships in the created order be more than they could possibly be for us (the infinite) is understandable given our deep desire for the infinite.

Whether we are thinking of two divorced persons suffering a loss of self-esteem, or other relationships in which one or both persons suffer this loss, they must first come to value themselves as loveable in and for themselves as well as knowing who they are apart from others if their relationship with one another is to succeed. On a deeper level we might interpret healthy self-love as a person being in touch with the mystery he or she is in his or her own eyes — or, to anticipate Jesus' image, a person is funded by something greater than the self, i.e., living water, the Source of the attraction which draws all of us toward Itself. To use an earlier image, we come to cherish one another and ourselves as echoes who come from The Voice, from God. Our reality is no more and no less.

But in her successive marriages the Samaritan woman becomes more and more desperate. Anyone offering the slightest possibility of satisfying her thirst she marries. However, now she also turns to "booze" and even endures physical abuse to satisfy her thirst. She had hoped she could have at least retained some semblance of dignity by not being called a slut as she repeatedly marries and remarries. But when she takes up living with a man not her husband she cannot avoid thinking herself a slut.

Living Waters

However, she reaches a turning point at the well when she meets Jesus. As biblical scholars have pointed out, it is noteworthy that

Jesus, a man and a Jew, initiates a conversation with this woman. This would have been enough to render Jesus unclean. However, he also asks for water from her bucket, another action religiously contaminating.

Significant, too, is that he speaks to her in a public space. Associating with her in this space would have been cause for scandal. But as scholars have pointed out, in the increasingly intimate dialogue between Jesus and this woman the public space is gradually transformed into private space, and within this space that usually occurred only with one's relatives, "fictive" or non-biological kinship occurs. By the time they have finished their conversation she will be a disciple belonging to Jesus' family.

Intuiting her desperation, Jesus observes that she married five times to satisfy her thirst. A few seconds later he speaks about the water in the well that doesn't quench her thirst just "like everything else we thirst for." He then suggests there is water in another well that satisfies completely and directs her attention to the water within herself. It is ready to bubble up and over parched land — obviously referring to the parched land of her own life.

His words touch her deeply as her tears flow, and she speaks openly about her life. "Let it flow! Let it flow," he cries. What is happening? Here I refer to a reflection I had written on another story about this woman when she began revealing what she had hidden even from herself for so many years.

> *For years persons might be able to avoid dealing with their anger, hurt feelings, pain, shame, and guilt, but then something happens. Someone is there for them and at first there may be just a trickle of resentment or anger or sadness that they experience. Merely trickles, but frightening signs since so long repressed. But then more and more feelings well up. And a well that's been capped for years yields distasteful water — muddy and stagnant — before the purer water is reached. Yet, it is necessary to reach in and let the negative distasteful feelings come up because in and through these feelings the person comes to experience oneself as "I am and it is good to be my self." When this experience of "I am"*

*happens the person has dropped the bucket deeply into
her well water. But there is more.*

*In the experience of going deeply into one's own
well is the possibility of recognizing that the water is
funded by a source beyond itself. "I am" will not dry
up because there is a power at the bottom of the well
which flows into and sustains all well water. It is that
power of which Jesus speaks when he tells the Samaritan woman she has a gift within. Her tears were signs
of that gift because there is continuity between the
simple welling up of tears and the power called the
Spirit. It is important that people who don't know what
they feel come to feel a feeling because it is a sign of
God's presence at the bottom of the well.*[5]

The connection constitutes well being. "I am and it is good to
be myself" is a journey from disowning the self, which is what the
woman did in the story by describing herself as always having
been a "has been." Now she can dwell fully within herself and
claim her worth as a person. But she also experiences the connection to the living waters or the source of her being, the source paradoxically which she had always longed for yet unbeknownst to her
was always closer to her than she was to herself. Saint Augustine
writes of a similar experience. When he seemed as far away from
God as he could possibly get he discovered that God was more
intimate to him than he was to himself.[6] Who could be closer to us
than we are to ourselves than God?

The meaning of experiencing a connection with the living
waters is enriched when we consider them from a depth psychological perspective. We have already seen in the story of Jonah and
the Good Samaritan that Carl Jung spoke of the center of the person as the Self. This Self refers both to unconscious and conscious
sides of the personality and their relationship with one another. In
this episode of the woman at the well the unconscious is symbolized as the maternal life-giving waters,[7] the Source from which we
derive new insight, vision, and direction for our lives. Immersion
in these waters signifies dying and rebirth. We die by returning to
these waters in order to achieve new vision and direction. This

return is not easy since it means encountering long-neglected feelings mentioned earlier, confronting shadowy, disowned sides of one's Self, but also connecting the person with something within the Self waiting to be born.

This process involves an initiation or new beginning that is ritually celebrated in a person's immersion in the life-giving waters of baptism. When Jesus offers the woman life-giving waters he is likewise mediating a connection to the Self. As I pointed out in the chapter on the Good Samaritan this Self is also imaged as the *imago dei* or the image of God. To be in touch with and touched by this deep Self is the psychological correlate of being touched by God.

This is a transition of major significance for the woman. While her marriages seem to have led her through transitions, they never led to any significant transformative changes. They were simply changes as when one rearranges the furniture from time to time in a room. Change in and of itself is not transformative. While she had been going through the motions of a transition or transformation the real transformation occurs in her encounter with Jesus.

He facilitates this transformation through his presence and his words. What she sees in and hears from him gradually leads her to admire him. At the beginning of their conversation she had pointed out the ethnic, gender, and religious difference between herself and Jesus. But as they continue she refers to him as sir, then prophet, and finally Messiah. During this whole process he is mirroring or mediating what she could not see in herself, someone whose worth is inestimable. Etymologically the words "admire, mirror, and miracle" are all related. The root words are the Latin *mirari* and *mirus*, from which come the words wonder at, astonishing, strange, wonderful, miracle, admire.[8] Thus she admires him even as he is mirroring her worth to herself, and in doing this is also mediating her depths, the living waters. The mediation of these living waters is the miracle at the well.

We might wonder what happens to her longing for the infinite if she is now in contact with these waters through Jesus' mediation. Being in touch with the source doesn't mean one's longing ceases. One can experience an even more profound longing for the

144

infinite to the degree that one has been profoundly touched by it. The difference between what she longed for before and after her encounter with Jesus is her growing awareness of what she was thirsting after during her journey. It was revealed to Saint Catherine of Sienna on her journey to God that she would not have found God had God not already found her. The discovery of God's already finding her prior to her finding God is a *celebration* of realizing God was present within from the beginning of her journey. So, too, for the woman at the well and for us, the living waters are present for those who look within. Still the taste of these living waters deepens our longing for the infinite. Stated otherwise, absence makes the heart grow fonder only because the heart is aware as never before whose touch of love it is.

Are there any dangers when one comes in contact with these living waters? Surprisingly, yes. It is possible to become puffed up or inflated by this experience. We might think ourselves superior to others because of what we have experienced. Spiritual hubris or pride inundates when we identify ourselves with the Source. It is as if the person touched by the infinite now acts as if he or she were the infinite. Perhaps that is why Saint Paul writes, "Love is patient; love is kind; love is not envious or boastful or arrogant or rude" (1 Corinthians 13:4-5). This leads us to consider what it meant for the woman to belong to Jesus' family.

Earlier I noted that Jesus included this woman in what the social scientists refer to as private space. She became an intimate member of his fictive family. It is belonging to Jesus' family that sustains and empowers one in the journey on one's longing for the infinite. The deeper the members connect with one another the more they are in touch with the living waters which funds all the wells. The Samaritan woman anticipates this as Jesus listens to her and in this listening she goes deeper and deeper within herself to these waters. She cannot claim these waters as her possession. She drops the bucket (a sign she is dropping everything to become a disciple), and hurries to the village to proclaim what has happened. Most likely she speaks to those who had kept their distance from her, but when she has finished testifying what happened at the well she draws others into Jesus' community through her witnessing. They will see for themselves who this Jesus is but they are already beginning to draw from the living waters within. The Messiah or Savior is already present through this woman's word and presence. Soon the villagers will become members of Jesus' family as she has. Here we might reflect on the importance of holding communities described in chapter 1 within the context of what happened at the well and among the villagers.

Jesus initiates the holding community as he listens to the woman. Through his presence he exercises the functions of the holding community that are: holding on, letting go, and enduring.

Holding On

He doesn't lecture her by telling her how she ought to feel or that she was foolish marrying five men, or that she should be thinking of all the good things that have happened to her. He is with her in her shame and guilt. He doesn't offer the Kleenex to stop her crying. He holds on by being present with her in the present moment.

Letting Go

However Jesus also lets go. He challenges her as he speaks of a future she might have by telling her of the living waters which give new life. What was can give way to what can be. He is there for her both as she is and who she can be.

Endures

And he endures as a holding community because he remains at the well as she goes to the village to tell the villagers about what happened between her and Jesus. Jesus himself will eventually go to the village and remain with them for two days (John 4:40).

Jesus mediates her worth as a person through his mirroring activity. The holding community continues Jesus' mirroring activity as they mirror back to one another a source beyond the person's self — living waters — as Jesus did to the woman at the well. We see Jesus in one another and ourselves when we see that "something else" in another which he has revealed. To see Christ in one another might then mean we see something else in each other, namely the depth dimension, the living waters which funds us all as uniquely revealed and mirrored back to us in Jesus. Mirroring for others what they were unaware of within themselves Jesus did what no one had or has ever done as he had done. By way of summary, we are always reaching for the infinite and we will always end up with less than the infinite. Our reach is greater than our grasp. In our grasping we often construct idols by demanding they be our gods. Periodically on our journey we need to be disillusioned and set free from demanding the finite be the infinite. Yet it would be misleading to suggest that if we were careful on our journey we would not construct idols at all. Still more misleading would it be if we concluded that we could connect directly with the living waters without first striving to satisfy our thirst with water at the well. The truth is the passion to quench our thirst for the eternal living waters draws us first to what is readily available or at hand, the well water. Then in and through tasting this water do we become aware of the inadequacy of this water to quench our thirst for something more, the life-giving water, the Source which funds all our wells.

Exercises

1. Has there ever been a time when you felt moved to tears because of some injustice you witnessed in the life or lives of people? Did you not only cry because of the injustice you witnessed but also went out of your way to right a wrong? Is it possible that the living waters of which Jesus spoke were in these tears you shed that led you to do something about an injustice? If you can recall any situation in which this occurred would you take a few minutes to write it down in your notebook?

2. Have you ever thought of your longing for something undefinable as a rumor of transcendence? Thus when you think of words like fascinating, enchanting, captivating, enveloping,

mesmerizing, do you realize that although they refer to something finite they seem to point to something beyond the finite which is the source of their being finite? "To be taken up," or "swept off one's feet," by these realities suggests ways in which we are touched by the divine. Can you recall any experiences you've had along these lines? Write one or two of these down. God might be beyond our definitions of God but we experience the traces of God's presence in our experience, as did the woman at the well when Jesus directed her to the living waters within. Is there any experience that you can recall that you would refer to as the living waters of which Jesus spoke?

Questions For Discussion

1. Do you more easily see God's hand at work in what is beautiful and marvelous than in moments when you are overwhelmed with grief over the loss of a loved one? What do spiritual writers mean by the gift of tears? Is it a reference to one's ability to stand in the shoes of the disenfranchised and marginalized of one's society, cry over what one sees, and is prompted to do something about it? Could these tears proceed from the living waters of which Jesus spoke?

2. When Jesus speaks of living waters bubbling up from within each of us, is he referring to the waters which run so deep within us that at a certain depth the personal merges with the transpersonal, i.e., the water funding one person's well is funding everyone's well and the connection with others is experienced at this level. Have you ever had the feeling of being at one with others so that their feelings could as easily be yours?

3. Isn't it interesting that when people speak of feeling dried up inside and of not feeling anything at all, anymore, that they often begin to cry? Are these tears an oasis in the middle of their desert? Are they life-giving waters ready to bubble up and over parched land?

1. Bruce J. Malina and Richrd L. Rohrbaugh, *Social-Science Commentary On The Synoptic Gospels* (Minneapolis: Fortress Press, 1992), pp. 98-102.

2. Carol A. Newsom and Sharon H. Ringe, ed., *Women's Bible Commentary* (Louisville: Westminster John Knox Press, 1998), pp. 381-384.

3. R. S. Pine trans. *Saint Augustine Confessions* (New York: Penguin Books, 1984), p. 21 (*fecisti nos at te et inquietem est cor nostrum, donec requiescat in te*).

4. Andre Papineau, *Jesus Stories For The Losers, The Lost And The Least* (Milwaukee: Lemieux International Ltd., 2001), pp. 104-109.

5. Andre Papineau, *Lightly Goes The Good News* (Lima, Ohio: CSS Publishing Company, 2002), p. 149.

6. Pine, *ibid.*, p. 121 (*tu autem eras interior intimo meo*).

7. J. E. Cirlot, *A Dictionary Of Symbols* (London: Routledge And Kegan Paul, 1976), pp. 364-367.

8. Eric Partridge, *Origins* (New York: Macmillian Publishing Company, Inc., 1966), p. 407.

Bibliography

Bailey, Kenneth E. *Through Peasant Eyes*. Grand Rapids, Michigan: Eerdmans, 1980.

Bellah, Robert, et alii, *Habits of the Heart*. Berkeley, California: University of California Press, 1985.

Berger, Peter. *A Rumor of Angels*. Garden City, New Jersey: Doubleday, 1969.

Berry, Wendell. "Health is Membership" *Utne Reader*, September-October, 1995.

Borg, Marcus. *Conflict, Holiness, And Politics In The Teaching Of Jesus*. Harrisburg, Pennsylvania: Trinity Press International, 1998.

Brown, Raymond. "Incidents That Are Units In The Synoptic Gospels But Dispersed in St. John," *Catholic Biblical Quarterly*, Vol. XXIII, No. 2, April, 1961.

Brown, Raymond. *An Introduction To The New Testament*. New York, New York: Doubleday, 1997.

Buttrick, David. *Speaking Parables: A Homiletic Guide*. Louisville, Kentucky: Westminster John Knox Press, 2000.

Cirlot, J. E. *A Dictionary Of Symbols*. London, England: Routledge And Kegan Paul, 1976.

Crossan, Dominic. *Jesus: A Revolutionary Biography*. San Francisco, California: HarperCollins, 1994.

D'Antonio, W. Y., Davidson, J. D., Hoge, D. R., Wallace, R. A. *Laity American And Catholic Transforming The Church*. Kansas City, Missouri: Sheed and Ward, 1996.

Donahue, John R. *The Gospel In Parable*. Minneapolis, Minnesota: Fortress Press, 1988.

Eisenberg, Ron. "Disease and Illness: Distinctions Between Professional and Popular Ideas of Sickness," *Culture, Medicine, and Psychiatry*, 1972.

Funk, Robert. *Honest To Jesus*. San Francisco, California: HarperCollins, 1997.

Gadow, Sally. "Touch and Technology: Two Paradigms of Patient Care," *Journal of Religion and Health,* Vol. 23, Spring, 1984.

Gill, Sam. "Disenchantment," *Parabola*, Summer, 1976.

Hegy, Pierre and Martos, Joseph, eds. *Catholic Divorce: The Deception of Annulments*. New York, New York: Continuum, 2000.

Hillman, James. "Betrayal" in *Loose Ends*. New York, New York: Spring Publications, 1995.

Howes, Elizabeth Boyden. *Jesus' Answer To God*. San Francisco, California: Guild For Psychological Studies Publishing House, 1984.

Hunt, G. W. "Of Many Things," *America* Magazine, June 18-25, 1994.

Kegan, Robert. *The Evolving Self.* Cambridge, Massachusetts: Harvard University Press, 1982.

Kennedy, Robert E. *Zen Spirit, Christian Spirit.* New York, New York: Continuum, 1999.

LaVerdiere, Eugene. *Dining In The Kingdom Of God.* Chicago, Illinois: Liturgy Training Publications, 1994.

Le Fevre, Carol and Le Fevre, eds. *Aging And The Human Spirit.* Chicago, Illinois: Exploration Press, 1981.

Levinson, Daniel. *The Seasons In A Man's Life.* New York, New York: Alfred A. Knopf, 1978.

Malina, Bruce J. and Rohrbaugh, Richard L. *Social-Science Commentary On The Synoptic Gospels.* Minneapolis, Minnesota: Fortress Press, 1992.

McKnight, John. *The Careless Society: Community And Its Counterfeits.* New York, New York: Basic Books, 1995.

Meier, John P. *A Marginal Jew*, Vol. 2. New York, New York: Doubleday, 1994.

Miller, Jean Baker. *Toward A New Psychology Of Women.* Boston, Massachusetts: Beacon Press, 1986.

Moore, Thomas. *Care Of The Soul.* San Francisco, California: HarperCollins, 1992.

Newsom, Carol A. and Ringe, Sharon H., eds. *Women's Bible Commentary.* (Louisville, Kentucky:Westminster /John Knox Press, 1998.

Neyrey, Jerome. "Idea of Purity in Mark's Gospel" in *Semeia 35.* Decatur, Georgia: Scholars Press, 1986.

Nouwen, Henri. *Care And The Elderly: Aging And The Human Spirit.* Chicago, Illinois: Exploration Press, 1975.

O'Connor, Elizabeth. *Our Many Selves*. New York, New York: Harper & Row, 1971.

Olen, Dale. *The Catholic Herald Press*. Milwaukee, Wisconsin.

O'Neill, Molly. "The Morality Of Fat" in *The New York Times* Magazine, March 10, 1996.

Papineau, Andre. *Breaking Up, Down And Through: Discovering Spiritual And Psychological Opportunities In Your Transitions*. Mahwah, New Jersey: Paulist Press, 1997.

Papineau, Andre. *Lightly Goes The Good News*. Lima, Ohio: CSS Publishing Company, Inc., 2002.

Papineau, Andre. *Jesus Stories For The Losers, The Lost And The Least*. Milwaukee, Wisconsin: Lemieux International Ltd., 2001.

Partridge, Eric. *Origins*. New York, New York: Macmillan Publishing Company, Inc., 1996.

Pine, R. S., trans. *Saint Augustine Confessions*. New York, New York: Penguin Books, 1984.

Real, Terrence. *How Can I Get Through To You?* New York, New York: Scribner, 2002.

Sanders, E. P. *Jesus And Judaism*. Philadelphia, Pennsylvania: Fortress Press, 1985.

Sanders, E. P. *The Historical Figure Of Jesus*. New York, New York: Penguin, 1995.

Sanford, John. "Jesus, Paul And Depth Psychology" in *Religious Education*, Vol. XLVIII, No. 6, November-December, 1973.

Steindl-Rast, David. "The Shadow In Christianity" in *Meeting The Shadow*. Los Angeles, California: Tarcher, 1991.

Thompson, Francis. *The Hound Of Heaven*. Harrisburg, Pennsylvania, 1998.

Watkins, Mary M. *Invisible Guests: The Development Of Imaginal Dialogues*.

Zweig, Connie. *The Holy Longing: The Hidden Power Of Spiritual Yearning*. New York, New York: Tarcher, 2003.